John
Paton

WOMEN OF FAITH SERIES

Amy Carmichael	*Hannah Whitall Smith*
Corrie ten Boom	*Isobel Kuhn*
Florence Nightingale	*Joni*
Gladys Aylward	*Mary Slessor*

MEN OF FAITH SERIES

Andrew Murray	*Jonathan Goforth*
Borden of Yale	*John Hyde*
Brother Andrew	*John Newton*
C. S. Lewis	*John Paton*
Charles Colson	*John Wesley*
Charles Finney	*Luis Palau*
Charles Spurgeon	*Martin Luther*
D. L. Moody	*Samuel Morris*
Eric Liddell	*Terry Waite*
George Muller	*William Booth*
Hudson Taylor	*William Carey*
Jim Elliot	

John and Betty Stam
Francis and Edith Schaeffer

John Paton

Benjamin Unseth

BETHANY HOUSE PUBLISHERS
MINNEAPOLIS, MINNESOTA 55438

John Paton
Copyright © 1996
Benjamin Unseth

Published by Bethany House Publishers
A Ministry of Bethany Fellowship, Inc.
11300 Hampshire Avenue South
Minneapolis, Minnesota 55438

Cover by Jessica Henry

Printed in the United States of America

Library of Congress Cataloging-in-Publication Data

Paton, John Gibson, 1824–1907.
   John Paton : missionary to the cannibals : his
autobiography / edited and abridged by Benjamin Unseth.
      p. cm. — (Men of faith)

   1. Paton, John Gibson, 1824–1907. 2. Missionaries—
Vanuatu—Biography. 3. Missionaries—Scotland—
Biography. 4. Vanuatu—Church history. 5. Missions—
Vanuatu. I. Unseth, Benjamin. II. Title. III. Series.
BV3680.N6P377   1996
266'.67'092—dc20
[B]   95–25925
ISBN 1–55661–495–0   CIP

To

Alec Brooks

who introduced me to John Paton

and to

Laurie Eve Loftin

who reintroduced me

BENJAMIN UNSETH'S previous works include editing *Jonathan Goforth* in the MEN OF FAITH series and major contributions to *The One-Minute Bible*. Since returning from Asia in 1989, he has trained missionaries and Bible translators at Moody Bible Institute, Wheaton College, and the Summer Institute of Linguistics—North Dakota. He lives in Chippewa Falls, Wisconsin, with his wife and children.

Contents

Vanuatu (The New Hebrides)

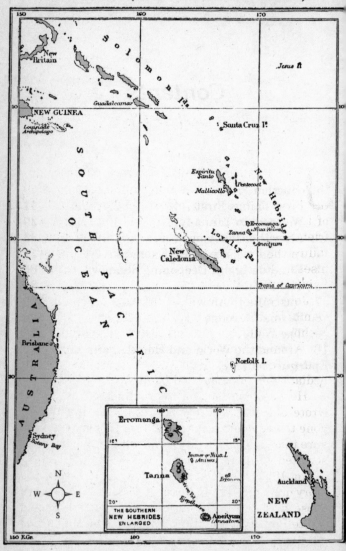

Introduction

J ohn Paton spent his life preaching to cannibals—when he was not running from them.
Charles Spurgeon introduced him as "the King
of the cannibals." Paton buried his family and
friends on the island of Tanna, escaping in seeming
failure. On neighboring Aniwa he endured similar
disease and danger, but there God gave birth to a
living church.

John Paton lectured at Princeton, Oxford, and
Cambridge Universities. He met lords, earls, archbishops, and two United States presidents. He
plays a significant role in mission history, rating a
four-page entry in Ruth Tucker's mission encyclo-
pedia, *From Jerusalem to Irian Jaya*.

He was renowned for his godliness. F. B. Meyer
wrote of Paton, "Surely he of all men must have
gone to heaven in a chariot of fire. It is such a pleasure to think that in any small way I have been associated with him."

In 1887 John Paton sat down and wrote the
story of his life—from birth, in 1824, to 1862. Since
those first 380 pages were so popular, he quickly
wrote Part Two—another 380 pages, on the period

9

of 1862–1885. A decade later he concluded his writing with Part Three, telling his story through 1898, another 100 pages. For this edition the original autobiography has been distilled to one-fifth of its original bulk. The language has been updated to remove the barriers of archaic vocabulary and grammar. Paton's New Hebrides islands are referred to under their modern name of Vanuatu.

Benjamin Unseth

1

First Things First

When pleading the cause of the lost and the claims of Jesus on His followers, I have often been touted as being "a man of one idea." Sometimes this has come from those who do not have even one idea—unless it is how to kill time or save their own skins. Seriously speaking, is it not better to have one good idea and to live for that and succeed in it than to scatter one's life away on many things and leave a mark on none?

Often I have had to run into a man's arms when his club was lifted or his musket leveled at my head. Praying to Jesus, I would cling to him so that he could neither strike nor shoot me till his anger cooled and I managed to slip away. Often I have seized the pointed barrel and directed it upward, or pleaded and struggled with my assailant till I uncapped his musket. At other times, nothing could be said, nothing done, but to stand still in silent prayer, asking God to protect me or to prepare me for going home to His glory. He has fulfilled His promise: I will never leave you or forsake you.

Once one of our Christian chiefs sent a message to an inland chief that he and four attendants

11

would come on Sunday and tell them the good news of Jehovah God. The reply threatened death to any Christian that approached the inland chief's village. Our chief sent back a loving message, telling him that Jehovah had taught the Christians to return good for evil, that they would come unarmed to tell them the story of how the Son of God came into the world and died in order to bless and save His enemies. The inland chief sent back a final reply: "If you come, you will be killed."

Sunday morning, the Christian chief and his four companions were met outside the village by the unbelieving chief, who threatened them once more.

"We come to you without weapons of war!" they told him. "We come only to tell you about Jesus. He will protect us today."

As they walked toward the village, spears began to fly at them. Some they evaded, all but one of the men being skilled warriors. Others they received with their bare hands and turned them aside in an incredible manner. The villagers were thunderstruck at the sight of these men approaching unarmed and not even flinging back the spears they had caught. They stopped from sheer surprise.

As our Christian chief and his friends joined their enemies on the village public ground, he called out, "Jehovah protects us. He has given us all your spears! Once we would have thrown them back at you and killed you. But now we come not to fight, but to tell you about Jesus. He has changed our dark hearts. He asks you now to lay down all your weapons of war and hear what we can tell you about the love of God, our great Father, the only living God."

They were awestruck. These Christians were clearly protected by some Invisible One. The villagers listened for the first time to the story of the gospel and of the Cross.

We lived to see that chief and all his tribe following Christ.

If there is much in my experience that the church of God ought to know, it would be pride on my part—not humility—to let it die with me. With that motive supreme in my heart, I lift my pen. What I write here is for the glory of God.

On the twenty-fourth of May, 1824, I was born near Dumfries, in southern Scotland. My parents raised me in Torthorwald, a thriving village of gardened cottages, their chimneys sending up blue peat smoke. Close by was the village school. Farther off, amid graves marked with crumbling stone dating back 500 years, the village church stood. Four miles behind it lay the ruins of the Castle of Bruce; a few miles in front of it, the still beautiful remains of Caerlaverock Castle. Traditions lost no power in their thousandth retelling by village patriarchs around the kindly peat fire, children gaping 'round. A certain glorious delight in daring enterprises was part of our common heritage.

Here my parents raised five sons and six daughters in a two-roomed thatched cottage. The house consists of three pairs of oak couples planted like solid trees in the ground at equal intervals, and gently sloped inward, meeting at the ridge, held together by great solid pins of oak. There it stands after not less than four centuries—the oak so hard that no ordinary nail can be driven through it, and perfectly capable of four centuries more!

Our home had two rooms with a closet in between. The one end was my mother's domain, and served as dining room, kitchen, parlor, and bedroom. Our grand, big, airy beds, were adorned with many-colored quilts and hung with curtains. The other end was my father's workshop, filled with five or six "stocking frames," whirring with the constant action of five or six pairs of busy hands and feet, and producing fine hosiery for merchants. The closet was a very small chamber between the two rooms, having space only for a bed, a little table, and a chair, with a tiny window shedding a ray of light on the scene.

After meals, we saw our father retire to the closet. Though the thing was too sacred to be talked about, we knew that prayers were being poured out there for us, for we occasionally heard his voice trembling and pleading. We learned to slip out and in past that door on tiptoe, not to disturb the holy communion. The outside world might not know, but we knew the source of that happy light that was always dawning on my father's face like a newborn's smile. It was a reflection from the Divine Presence. Though everything else of religion was by some unthinkable catastrophe to be swept away from memory, my soul would shut itself up in that sanctuary closet, and hearing still the echoes of those cries to God would hurl back all doubt with the victorious appeal, "He walked with God, why not I?"

———————

Our mother, while a young woman caring for her old uncle and aunt, noticed a young stocking maker, James Paton. My father was in the habit of stealing alone into the quiet wood, book in hand, day after day, at certain hours, as if for private study and meditation. It was a very excusable curiosity that led the young bright heart of the girl to watch him devoutly reciting Ralph Erskine's "Gospel Sonnets," laying aside his broad hat, kneeling down under the wings of some tree, and pouring out all his soul in daily prayers to God. As yet they had never spoken.

One day she slipped in quietly, stole his hat and hung it on a branch nearby while his trance of devotion made him oblivious of all around. From a safe retreat she watched and enjoyed his perplexity in seeking and finding it! A second day this was repeated, but his long pondering with the hat in his hand, as if almost alarmed, touched another chord in her heart. Next day, when he came to his accustomed place of prayer, a little card was pinned against the tree just where he knelt, and on it these words: "She who stole away your bonnet is ashamed of what she did. She has a great respect for you, and asks you to pray for her that she may become as good a Christian as you."

Staring long at that writing, he forgot Ralph Erskine for one day. Taking down the card, and wondering who the writer could be, he scolded himself for his stupidity in wondering whether angels had come during his prayer. Suddenly raising his eyes, he saw among the trees the passing of another kind of angel, swinging a milk pail in her hand and merrily singing some snatch of an old Scottish song.

He knew that she must be his angel visitor, that bright-faced, clever-witted niece of his neighbors.

Somewhere around his seventeenth year, my father passed through a crisis of religious experience, and from that day he openly followed the Lord Jesus. None of us can remember that any day ever passed without Scripture reading and Father's voice softly joining in singing a psalm and his lips breathing morning and evening prayers—sweet benediction falling on the heads of all his children. No hurry for market, no rush to business, no arrival of friends or guests ever prevented at least our kneeling around the family altar, while our high priest led our prayers to God and offered himself and his children there. The worst woman in the village declared that the only thing that kept her from suicide was creeping close up underneath my father's window in the dark winter nights to hear him praying, pleading, in family worship. "I felt," she said, "that I was a burden on that good man's heart, and I knew that God would not disappoint *him*. That thought kept me out of hell, and at last led me to the only Savior."

We loved him all the more when we saw how much it cost him to punish us. If we did anything seriously wrong, Father went first to his closet for prayer, and we knew that he was laying the whole matter before God. That was the severest part of the punishment for me to bear! I could have defied any amount of mere penalty, but this spoke to my conscience as a message from God.

At sickbeds and at funerals he was constantly sent for. This appreciation greatly increased when years whitened his long, flowing locks, and in the last twelve years of his life he served as a rural missionary.

One evening, when my father was leading the family in prayer, the door of our house gently opened and closed again. Rushing to the door after prayer, I found a parcel containing a new suit of warm and excellent clothes. At school the next morning, the teacher cheerily complimented me on my fine clothes. I innocently told him how they had arrived, and he laughingly replied, "John, whenever you need anything after this, just tell your father to 'take the Book,' and God will send it in answer to prayer!" Years passed by before I came to know that the good-hearted schoolmaster's hand had lifted the latch that evening. His influence, however, was marred by occasional bursts of fierce and ungovernable temper. Once, after he had flogged me unjustly, I returned to school only by my mother's plea. He apologized to my parents but nothing would induce me to continue my studies there.

Though under twelve years of age, having quit school, I started to learn my father's trade in which I made surprising progress. We worked from six in the morning till ten at night, with an hour break for dinner and half an hour for breakfast and again at supper. These spare moments every day I spent in my books, chiefly in Latin and Greek. I had given my soul to God and was resolved to become a missionary or a minister.

Potato and other crops failed, and our family, like all others peasants, felt the financial pinch severely. When our father was gone to sell our goods, the meal barrel ran empty, and our dear mother coaxed us all to rest. She assured us that she had told God everything, and that He would send us plenty in the morning. Next day a present came in the mail from her father. Knowing nothing of her circumstances or of this trial, he had been moved by God to send at that particular time a love offering to his daughter. My mother, seeing our surprise at such an answer to her prayers, took us around her knees and thanked God for His goodness and encouraged us to trust Him.

I saved enough at my trade to go six weeks to Dumfries Academy. This reawakened in me the hunger for learning, and I resolved to give up the trade and turn to something that would help in my education. Next, I secured work with a surveying crew. Instead of spending the midday hour with the rest at football and other games, I stole away to a quiet spot on the riverbank and there pored over my books, all alone. Our supervisor, unknown to me, had observed this from his house on the other side of the stream. After a time he called me into his office and inquired what I was studying. I told him the whole truth as to my desires. He then promised me a promotion in the service and special training at the government's expense, on condition that I would sign an engagement for seven years. Thanking him most gratefully for his kind offer, I agreed to bind myself for three or four years, but not for seven.

He retorted, "Why? Will you refuse an offer that many gentlemen's sons would be proud of?"

"My life is given to another Master," I said, "so I cannot engage myself for seven years."

"To whom?" he asked sharply.

"To the Lord Jesus, and I want to prepare as soon as possible for His service in proclaiming the Gospel."

My supervisor sprang across the room in great anger and exclaimed, "Accept my offer, or you are dismissed on the spot!"

"I am extremely sorry if you dismiss me," I answered, "but to bind myself for seven years would frustrate the purpose of my life; and though I am greatly obliged to you, I cannot make such a commitment." He gave me my pay without further discussion.

After working on a farm for harvest I received an offer to interview for a position as district visitor and tract distributor among Sunday school absentees. It included the privilege of receiving one year's schooling to qualify for teaching, a step toward the holy ministry. Two days later, I started out for Glasgow. The first forty miles had to be made on foot, and then the remainder by rail. A small bundle tied up in my pocket handkerchief held my Bible and all my personal belongings.

My dear father walked with me the first six miles of the way. His counsel and tears on that parting journey are fresh in my heart as if it had been yesterday. Tears are on my cheeks as freely now as then. For the last half mile we walked in almost unbroken silence, my father, as was often his custom, carrying his hat in hand, his long, flowing yellow hair streaming down his shoulders. His lips kept moving in silent prayers for me, and his tears fell fast when our eyes met. We halted upon reaching the appointed parting place. He grasped my hand firmly for a minute in silence, and then solemnly and affectionately said, "God bless you, my son! Your father's God prosper you, and keep you from all evil!"

Unable to say more, his lips kept moving in silent prayer. In tears we embraced, and parted. I ran off as fast as I could. When about to turn a corner in the road where he would lose sight of me, I looked back and saw him still standing with head uncovered where I had left him. Waving my hat goodbye, I was 'round the corner and out of sight in an instant. But my heart was too full and sore to carry me farther, so I darted to the side of the road and wept for a time. Rising up cautiously, I climbed the dyke to see if he yet stood where I had left him. Just at that moment I caught a glimpse of him climbing the dyke and looking out for me! He did not see me, and after he had gazed eagerly in my direction for a while, he got down, turned his face toward home, and began to return. I watched through blinding tears till his form faded from my gaze. Hastening on my way, I vowed deeply and often to live and act so as never to grieve or dishonor such a father and mother as God had given me.

In Glasgow I discovered I was one of two candidates for the position. The examiners suggested that one of us could withdraw in favor of the other. However, since we were both persistent, they decided to split the small yearly salary between us and pay the seminary fees for both of us. By dividing the mission work, we had more time for study. We soon realized our fellow students were all far advanced beyond us, and we found it exhausting work. Grinding away late and early, both of us broke down in health, partly because of hard study, but principally for lack of a nourishing diet. A severe cough seized me, and I began spitting blood. A doctor ordered me home to the country at once. It was a dreadful disappointment. Soon after, my friend became just as ill. Though stronger than I, he never fully recovered and long ago fell asleep in Jesus.

After a short rest in the hill air of Torthorwald, drinking the milk of our family cow, I was at work again, teaching at a small school. After saving a little money I returned to Glasgow and enrolled again. But before the session was finished my money was gone; I had lent some to a poor student who failed to repay me. No course seemed open for me except to give up my college career and seek teaching or other work in the country.

I wrote a letter to my father and mother. But having read the letter over again through many tears, I said, "I cannot send it. It will grieve my darling parents. Leaving it on the table, I locked my door and went out to sell my few precious books in order to hold on a few weeks longer. Then a notice in a window caught my eye: Teacher wanted, Maryhill Free Church School. I jumped a coach just passing, called on the minister, and accepted the position. I paid my landlady, tore up the letter to my parents, and wrote another full of cheer and hope.

Early the next morning I started at the school. The minister warned me, however, that the school was in shambles. Coarse characters from the mills and coal pits attended evening classes and had abused several masters in succession. Laying a heavy cane on the desk, he said, "Use it freely, or you will never keep order here!"

There were very few scholars the first week, eighteen in the day school and twenty in the evenings. The mill clerk came to the evening classes to guard me from personal injury. The following week a young man and woman came to the night school bent on mischief. With my repeated appeals for quiet and order they became even more boisterous. I urged the young man, a tall, powerful fellow, to be quiet or leave, declaring that at all cost I must and would have perfect order. He only mocked me and assumed a fighting position. Quietly locking the door and putting the key in my pocket, I took the cane from the desk. The student swung at me clumsily with his fists. I evaded him with quick movements and dealt him blow after blow with the heavy cane for several rounds. At length he crouched down at his desk, exhausted and beaten, and I ordered him to turn to his book, which he did in sulky silence.

The next morning, two of the bigger boys in the day school got in under the floor where coal and lumber were kept and made noises that sounded as if a dog and cat were clawing at each other. I appointed the other children in the classroom as jury to hear the case and to pass sentence. The two were found guilty and a severe lashing was declared the appropriate discipline. I proposed, as this was their first offense, to forego all punishment, if they apologized and promised to be attentive and obedient in the future. They both heartily did so and became my favorite scholars.

Before long the cane became a forgotten instrument; the disappointment and pain I showed for poorly done lessons, or anything blameworthy, proved the far more effective penalty. The school prospered. Its committee, regarding my arrangement as temporary, took advantage of the larger attendance and improved reputation to secure the services of a master of the highest caliber.

Before teaching at the school, I had applied as an agent for the Glasgow City Mission. The night before I had to leave the school, I received a letter from the head of the Mission. The directors had kept their eyes on me and asked if I would appear before them the next morning to be examined as a missionary. Praising God, I went off at once, passed the examination, and spent two hours that afternoon and the next Monday in visitation with two of the directors. We called at every house in a low district of the town, talking with everyone we met about their eternal welfare. After preaching a trial message in a mission meeting, I was unanimously appointed as a city missionary.

Looking back on these city mission experiences, I have always felt that they were to me and many others good training for the ministry. It prepared me to deal with people of every shade of thought and character, and endeavor to lead them to the knowledge and service of the Lord Jesus.

They sent me to start a new work around Green Street of Calton. I was expected to spend four hours daily visiting from house to house, holding small prayer meetings, calling the people together for evening meetings, and trying by all means to do whatever good was possible among them. The only place in the whole district available for a Sunday evening evangelistic service was a hayloft over a cow barn, which had to be reached by a rickety wooden stair outside.

After nearly a year's hard work there were only six or seven who had been led to attend regularly, besides the same number who met an evening a week in a home. The directors proposed to move me to another district. At our next meeting, I informed our small assembly that I would be sent to another part of the city if we could not together draw out more non-churchgoers to attend the services. With that announcement, each one then and there agreed to bring another person along to our next meeting.

Both meetings doubled at once in attendance. Then, for fear I might still be taken away, they doubled the attendance again by the next meeting. Soon the classes and meetings became too large for any house available to us in the whole district. We began a Bible class, a singing class, a new church member class, a liquor abstinence society, a mutual improvement society for men, and two prayer meetings specially for the Calton division of the Glasgow Police—one for the day shift and one for the night shift. My work now occupied every evening in the week, and I had two meetings every Sunday. By God's blessing they all prospered and showed the fruit of His working there with us as His humble instruments.

A church campus with school buildings and a house came on to the market, and was soon purchased for me to conduct all my meetings. The halls were adapted as schools for poor girls and boys, where they were educated and given clothing and even food. Every Sunday morning I led a Bible study for seventy to one hundred of the very poorest young women and men of the whole district. They had nothing to wear except their ordinary working clothes—all without hats, some without shoes. My delight in that Bible class was among the purest joys in all my life, and the results were among the clearest and precious of all my ministry. Eight young lads of humble circumstances educated themselves for the ministry of the church. From five to six hundred people attended weekly meetings, consisting of poor workers, largely the poorest class of mill workers. Several Christian employers offered to give employment to every deserving person recommended by me, and that relieved much distress and greatly increased my influence for good.

Almost the only enemies I had were the keepers of taverns, whose trade had been damaged by my liquor abstinence society. They tried to break up an outdoor meeting and even had me arrested once. In Catholic areas there was great opposition. A young Catholic woman who joined us was kidnapped, imprisoned, and left to die at the poorhouse. I was sent death threats. A well-thrown stone cut me severely above the eye. Attempts were made to pour pails of boiling water on my head, over windows and down dark stairs, but in every case I miraculously escaped.

All through my city mission tenure I was painfully carrying on my studies, first at the University of Glasgow, and then at the Reformed Presbyterian Divinity Hall, and also medical classes at the Andersonian College. With the exception of one session, when my health failed, I struggled patiently on through ten years. I was sustained by the lofty aim to preach the gospel of Christ, to be owned and used by Him for the salvation of perishing men and women.

My church body had been advertising for another missionary to join the Reverend John Inglis in his work in Vanuatu [the New Hebrides]. For two years their appeal had failed. The Lord kept saying within me, "Since none better qualified can be found, rise and offer yourself!" But I was dreadfully afraid of mistaking my own emotions for the will of God. The wail and the claims of the lost were constantly sounding in my ears. None seemed prepared for the foreign field; many were capable and ready for the Calton service. My medical studies as well as my linguistic and divinity training had especially qualified me in some ways for the foreign field. The voice within me sounded like a voice from God.

I offered myself for the Vanuatu mission and returned to my room with a lighter heart than I had for some time enjoyed. Nothing so clears the vision and lifts the heart as a decision to move forward in what you know to be entirely the will of the Lord. I said to my fellow student, who had been my friend all through college, "I have been away signing my banishment. I have offered myself as a missionary for Vanuatu."

After a long and silent meditation he answered, "If they will accept me, I also am resolved to go!" A few minutes later his letter of offer was in the mail. Next morning, the mission director called on us early, and after a long conversation, commended us and our future work to the Lord God in fervent prayer.

My friend Joseph Copeland had also been a very successful city missionary for some time while attending along with me at the Divinity Hall. This leading of God, whereby we both resolved at the same time to give ourselves to the foreign mission field, was wholly unexpected. We had never once spoken to each other about going abroad. For the next twelve months we were placed under a special committee for advice as to medical experience, learning the basics of trades, and anything else that might be useful to us in the foreign field.

Nearly all were dead set against my going abroad as a missionary, except the mission director and my friend Joseph. My dear father and mother neither discouraged nor encouraged me. Even my own pastor, a professor in the seminary, repeatedly urged me to remain at home. He argued, "Green Street Church is doubtless the sphere for which God has given you peculiar qualification, and in which He has so largely blessed your labors. You would only throw your life away among cannibals."

"Though I love my work and my people," I replied, "yet I feel that I can leave them to the care of Jesus, who will soon provide them a better pastor than I. With regard to my life among the cannibals, as I have only once to die, I am content to leave the time, place, and means in the hands of God."

A parsonage and generous salary were now offered to me, on condition that I remain at home. One dear old Christian gentleman repeatedly exhorted me, "The cannibals! You will be eaten by cannibals!"

At last I replied, "Mr. Dickson, you are advanced in years now, and your own prospect is to soon be laid in the grave, there to be eaten by worms. I confess to you that if I can but live and die serving and honoring the Lord Jesus, it will make no difference to me whether I am eaten by cannibals or by worms. And in the great day my resurrection body will arise as fair as yours in the likeness of our risen Redeemer."

My dear Green Street people daily pleaded with me to remain. Indeed, the opposition was so strong from nearly all, and many of them warm Christian friends, that I was sorely tempted to question whether I was carrying out God's will or only some headstrong wish of my own. I again laid the whole matter before my dear parents, and they urged me to go:

"We feared to bias you, but now we must tell you why we praise God for the decision to which you have been led. Your father's heart was set on being a minister, but other claims forced him to give it up. When you were given to us, your father and mother laid you upon the altar, their firstborn, to be consecrated, if God saw fit, as a missionary of the Cross. It has been our constant prayer that you might be prepared, qualified, and led to this very decision. We pray with all our heart that the Lord may accept your offering, long spare you, and give you many souls from the lost for your service."

From that moment every doubt as to my path of duty forever vanished. As to a minister for Green Street, my brother Walter gave up a good business position and carried forward the Green Street Mission.

My future clear, I married an educated, consecrated young woman named Mary Ann Robson.

2

Welcome to Tanna

Another missionary candidate and I spent four months visiting and addressing nearly every congregation and Sunday school in the Reformed Presbyterian Church of Scotland that the people might see us and know us and take a personal interest in our work. On the twenty-third of March, 1858, we were ordained as ministers of the gospel and set apart as missionaries to Vanuatu. On the sixteenth of April we set sail for Australia and then to the island of Aneityum, where we arrived August 30. We received a hearty welcome from all our new friends, the missionaries and Christian natives of this South Sea island. Soon after, a meeting was called to consult about our settlement, and by the advice of all, Mr. and Mrs. Mathieson from Nova Scotia were located on the south side of Tanna at Kwamera and my wife and I at Port Resolution on the same island.

These islands comprise a range of mountains bursting up out of the sea, clothed with forests, and severed from each other by deep valleys, through which the tides flow. They are all volcanic in origin, but the lava has poured itself out over a bed of coral, and the mountains have reared themselves up on a coral base. The volcanic fires are still active on Tanna, Ambrym, and Polevi. The volcano on Tanna is now, as in the days of Captain Cook, a pillar of cloud by day and of fire by night, a far-shining lighthouse for the sailor, kindled by the finger of God himself. The climate is moist and humid, with a temperature seldom below 60 degrees Fahrenheit and seldom above 90 degrees Fahrenheit. Their winter is a rainy season, and their vegetation is tropical and luxuriant.

Dr. Inglis and a number of natives accompanied us to Tanna. We purchased a site for Mathiesons' mission house and church at Kwamera and began construction on their home. Then we went on to Port Resolution, and again purchased land and started a house, this one for my wife and me.

My first impressions drove me to the verge of utter dismay. Landing on Tanna we found the people there to be literally naked and painted: the women wore only a tiny apron of grass, in some cases shaped like a skirt or girdle; the men wore an indescribable affair, like a pouch or bag; and the children absolutely nothing whatsoever! My heart was as full of horror as pity. Had I given up my much-beloved work and my dear friends in Glasgow to devote my life to these degraded creatures? Was it possible to teach them right from wrong, to bring them to Christ? Even to civilize them?

Soon, however, I was as deeply interested in them as ever I had been in my work at Glasgow. We had been surprised and delighted to see the remarkable change God had worked in the people of Aneityum in so short a time. By prayerful perseverance in the use of similar methods to those the missionaries on Aneityum used, we hoped to see the same work of God repeated on Tanna.

One day two hostile tribes met near our station. Strong words were exchanged and old feuds revived. The inland people withdrew, and the harbor people rushed past us in pursuit of their enemies, muskets discharging. Excitement and terror showed on every face. Armed men hurried in every direction—feathers in their twisted hair; faces painted red, black, and white, some with one cheek black and the other red, others with brow white and chin blue. Some of the women ran with their children to safety. Other girls and women, on the shore close by, chewed sugar cane, chatted, and laughed, as if their fathers and brothers were engaged in a country dance instead of a bloody conflict.

In the afternoon, as the sounds of the muskets and the yelling of the warriors came unpleasantly near, Dr. Inglis, leaning against a post for a little while in silent prayer, said, "The walls of Jerusalem were built in troubled times, and why not the mission house on Tanna? But let us rest for this day and pray for these poor, lost people."

We retired to a native house and pleaded before God for them all. We learned later that five or six men had been killed that day, their bodies cooked and eaten that very night less than a mile from us.

The next evening, as we sat talking, the night quiet was broken by a wild wailing cry from the villages around, long continued and unearthly. A man wounded in the battle had just died, and his own tribesmen had strangled his widow to death so that her spirit might accompany him to the other world,

his servant there as she had been here. Our hearts
sank to think of all this happening within earshot.

———

Having done all we could for lack of lime and
sawn wood to finish the mission house, we made an
agreement with the Tannese for knives, calico, and
axes, in exchange for their burning lime and preparing other things for our return. We hurried back
to Aneityum to finish preparations. We wanted to
get settled on Tanna before the rainy season set in.

My wife and I arrived together on Tanna the
fifth of November, 1858. At first the Tannese came
in crowds to look at us and at everything we did or
had. We knew nothing of their language. We could
not speak a single word to them nor they to us. We
smiled and nodded and made signs to each other;
this was our first meeting and parting. One day a
man lifted up one of our things and said to his
friend, *"Nunksi nari enu?"*

I guessed that he was asking, "What is this?" Instantly lifting a piece of wood, I repeated, *"Nunksi
nari enu?"*

They smiled and spoke to each other. I understood them to be saying, "He has got hold of our language now." Then they told me their name for the
thing that I had pointed to. I found that they understood my question "What is this?" I could now
get the name of everything around us! We carefully
noted every name they gave us, spelling all phonetically, and making special notes on each strange
sound. By painstaking comparison of different circumstances, we tested our own guesses by cross-
questioning the islanders. One day I saw two males

approaching. One, a stranger, pointed at me and said, *"Se nangin?"*

Concluding that he was asking my name, I pointed to one of them, and looking at the other, asked, *"Se nangin?"* They smiled and gave me their names. Now we were able to get the names of both things and persons. Our ears became familiarized with the distinctive sounds of their language. We made extraordinary progress in attempting bits of conversation and in reducing their speech to a written form for the first time.

Among our most interested and trustworthy language helpers were two aged chiefs—Nowar and Nouka—two of nature's noblest gentlemen, kind at heart to all and with certain dignity. But they were both under the leadership of the war chief Miaki, a kind of devil king over many villages and tribes. He and his brother were the recognized leaders in all dark deeds. They gloried in bloodshed, war, and cannibalism.

The Tannese had hosts of stone idols, charms, and sacred objects which they deeply feared and devoutly worshiped. Their religion was entirely a service of fear, its aim being to satisfy this or that evil spirit in order to prevent calamity or to get revenge. So far as I ever learned, they had no idea of a God of mercy or grace. Almost every village or tribe had its own sacred man, and some had many. These village and tribal priests were believed to control life and death through their ceremonies, not only in their own tribe, but over all the islands. Sacred men and women, wizards and witches, regularly received presents to influence the gods—to remove sickness or to cause it by *nahak,* cursing people by incantation over the remains of their food, or the skin of fruit they had eaten, such as banana peels.

Not being able to live without some sort of god, they have made idols of almost everything: trees and groves, rocks and stones, springs and streams, insects and animals, men and departed spirits, relics such as hair and fingernails, the heavenly bodies and volcanos. Every being and everything within their range of vision or knowledge they appealed to as god, clearly showing that human instinct, however degraded, calls us to worship and lean on some being or power outside ourselves and greater than ourselves.

The fact that they did worship, believed in an invisible world of spirits, and cherished legends of heroes they had never seen made it easier to teach them about the Lord who created and sustains all that is. The Tannese called heaven by the name Aneai; we learned that this was the name of the highest and most beautifully situated village on the island. The finest place they knew on Earth was to them a symbol of heaven. The fact that they had an Aneai, a promised land, opened their minds naturally to the Bible's promised land of the future. The universal craving to know the greater and more powerful gods, and to have them on their side, led them to listen eagerly to all our stories about Jehovah God, His Son Jesus, and all the mighty works recorded in the Bible.

But when we began to teach them that this almighty and living Jehovah God was calling them to throw away their idols and stop their wrongdoing, they rose in anger and cruelty against us. They persecuted everyone who was friendly to the mission.

Our story is the old battle of history: light had attacked darkness in its very stronghold, and it seemed that the light would be eclipsed, and that God's day would never dawn on Tanna!

—————

A glance backward over the story of the Gospel in Vanuatu will help in understanding the events to follow. Williams and Harris were among the earliest to attempt to introduce Christianity among this group of islands in the South Pacific seas. They landed on Erromanga on the thirtieth of November, 1839. Within a few moments of touching land, both were clubbed to death. The Erromangans cooked and feasted on their bodies. In this way Vanuatu was baptized with the blood of martyrs, thus announcing to the whole Christian world that Christ had claimed these islands as His own.

In 1842, Turner and Nisbet placed their standard on Tanna, the nearest island to Erromanga. In less than seven months their persecution became so dreadful that they were forced to flee for their lives, leaving by boat in the middle of the night.

Next, Christian teachers from Samoa came to one and another island in Vanuatu, but sickness and persecution discouraged them and they returned home to Samoa.

Rev. John Geddie and his wife, from Nova Scotia, landed on Aneityum, the most southerly island of Vanuatu, in 1848. Scottish missionaries Rev. John Inglis and his wife landed on the other side of Aneityum in 1852. The natives of Aneityum showed interest in the missionaries from the very first. In a few years the Inglises and Geddies saw about

3,500 Aneityumese throw away their idols and pledge themselves to worship the true Jehovah God. Every household on the island observed family worship; God's blessing was asked on every meal; peace and public order were secured; and property was perfectly safe—all this from the sanctifying and civilizing Gospel of Christ.

These missionaries lived to see the whole Bible, which they worked on with my friend Joseph Copeland, translated and published. These Aneityumese, having glimpses of this Word of God, determined to have the Holy Bible in their mother tongue. The missionaries kept toiling day and night in translating God's Book; the willing hands and feet of the islanders worked fifteen long but unwearying years, planting and preparing arrowroot to pay for the printing of the Book. Year after year the arrowroot, too sacred to be used for their daily food, was set apart as the Lord's portion. Let those who lightly esteem their Bibles think on this. Fifteen years of income did not appear too much to pay for the Word of God.

Our first house on Tanna was on the old site occupied by Turner and Nisbet, near the shore and only a few feet above the tide mark. The Mathiesons' home was also handy for materials and goods being landed, and close to the sea breezes. But the sites proved to be hotbeds for fever and ague, mine especially, and much of this might have been avoided by building on higher ground in the sweep of the refreshing trade winds.

My dear young wife, Mary Ann, and I landed on Tanna the fifth of November, 1858, in excellent health and full of holy hope. On the twelfth of February, 1859, she gave birth to our son; for two days or so both mother and child seemed to prosper. My darling had had an attack of ague and fever a few days before the birth, and on the third day afterward, it returned and attacked her with increasing severity every second day for two weeks. Diarrhea ensued and symptoms of pneumonia, with slight delirium at intervals. In a moment, unexpectedly, she died on March 3. Her last words were, "You must not think that I regret coming here. If I had the same thing to do over again, I would do it with far more pleasure, yes, with all my heart."

To crown my sorrows and complete my loneliness, our dear baby boy, Peter Robert Robson Paton, was taken from me after one week's sickness, on March 20. Let those who have ever passed through any similar midnight darkness feel for me; as for all others, it would be more than vain to try to paint my sorrows!

Stunned by my dreadful losses, my reason seemed for a time almost to give way. Ague and fever laid a depressing and weakening hand upon me, reaching the very height of its worst burning stages. The ever merciful Lord sustained me to lay the precious dust of my beloved ones in the same quiet grave, which I dug for them at the end of the house. I built the grave round and round with coral blocks and covered the top with beautiful white coral, broken small. That spot became my sacred and much-frequented shrine during the following months and years as I labored on for the salvation of these fierce islanders. With ceaseless prayers and tears I claimed that land for God in which I had buried my dead with faith and hope. But for Jesus, and the fellowship He gave me there, I would certainly have gone mad and died beside that lonely grave.

3

After the Honeymoon

The novelty of our being among the Tannese soon passed away, and they began to show their avarice and deceitfulness in every possible way. The chiefs united and refused to give us half of the small piece of land we had purchased. When we attempted to fence in the part they had left to us, they threatened our Aneityumese teachers and us with death if we proceeded. I paid as they demanded, and for a little season they appeared to be friendly again.

After these events, a few weeks of dry weather began to tell against the growth of their yams and bananas. The drought was instantly ascribed to us and our God. The islanders far and near were summoned to consider the matter in public assembly. The next day, Nouka, the high chief, and Miaki, the war chief, Nouka's nephew, came to inform us of the assembly's decisions: Two powerful chiefs had openly declared that if the harbor people did not kill us at once or compel us to leave the island, they would—unless the rain came plentifully in the meantime. They would summon all the inland people and murder both of us and our harbor chiefs.

Nouka and Miaki said, "Pray to your Jehovah God for rain, and do not go far beyond your door for a time. We are all in the greatest danger, and if war breaks out we fear we cannot protect you."

The following Sunday, just when we were assembling for worship, rain began to fall, and it rained heavily. Everyone believed that it was sent to save us in answer to our prayers. They called another assembly and resolved to let us remain on Tanna. The continuous and heavy rains, however, brought much sickness and fever, and again their sacred men pointed to us as the cause. Hurricane winds blew and injured their fruit trees, another opportunity to blame the missionaries and their Jehovah God.

After Sunday morning service we used to walk many miles, visiting all the villages within reach, even before we knew much of their language. Sometimes we made a circuit among them ten or twelve villages away and as many back again. We tried to talk a little to all who were willing to listen, and we conducted the worship of Jehovah wherever we could find two or three willing to gather together and to sit or kneel beside us. It was tiring work and in many ways disheartening. But it did help us to see the people and to get acquainted with the surrounding districts. It also secured for us considerable audience except when they were at war.

No real progress could be made in conveying spiritual knowledge to them till we had attained some familiarity with their language. We soon found out that there were two distinct languages spoken in and around Port Resolution, but we confined ourselves to the one understood by those closest to us, and our co-laborers at the other mission house did the same for their region.

When one of my Aneityumese teachers and Mr. Mathieson on the other side of Tanna both became sick and died, the islanders demanded me to tell them the cause of the deaths: Whose fault was it? Other reasoning or explanation proving useless, I turned the tables and demanded them to tell me why all this trouble and death had overtaken us in their land, whether they themselves were not the cause of it all? This simple question turned the whole current of their speculations. They held meeting after meeting for several days just to discuss it and then sent this message: "We do not blame you, and you must not blame us for causing these troubles and death. We believe that a bushman must have got hold of a portion of something we ate and thrown it to the great evil spirit in the volcano, thereby bringing all these troubles and curses."

However, when an old visiting chief died and his brother became sick, everyone blamed us. The Tannese became furious. This was proof that we were the cause of their sickness and death. Inland and all along the other side of the island everyone was enjoying excellent health. Meeting after meeting was held with exciting speeches and great feasts. For the feasts several women were sacrificed, cooked, and eaten. It was publicly resolved that a band of men be selected and commissioned to kill all those friendly to the mission. Frenzy prevailed, and the blood fiend seemed to override the whole assembly. Then under an impulse that surely came from the Lord of Pity, one great warrior chief who had kept his silence rose, swung high a mighty club and smashed it to the ground, crying aloud, "The man that kills

Missi must first kill me. The men that kill the mission teachers must first kill me and my people. We shall stand by them and defend them till death."

Instantaneously another chief thundered in with the same declaration, and the great assembly broke up in dismay. This deliverance was all the more remarkable because these two chiefs, as disease makers and sacred men, were regarded among our most bitter enemies. Once, when a brother of the first chief was wounded in battle, I had dressed his wounds and he recovered. Perhaps the chief now favored us for that deed, but I thanked the Lord.

The excitement did not at once subside. Men continued to club and beat their women for the smallest offenses. At every opportunity I denounced their conduct and rebuked them severely, especially one wretch who beat his wife right in front of our house, as well as one of the women who tried to protect her. On the following day he returned with an armed band and threatened our lives. I stood up in front of their weapons and firmly condemned their conduct, telling that man particularly that his conduct was evil and cowardly. At length his anger broke. He dropped his club in a penitent mood and promised to refrain from such evil ways.

On Tanna, the woman is the slave of man. She is kept working hard and bears all the heavier burdens while he walks by her side with musket, club, or spear. If she offends him he beats or abuses her at will. Such scenes were so common that no one thought of interfering. Even if the woman died in his hands, or immediately afterward, neighbors took little notice. And their children were so little cared for that my constant wonder was how any of them survived at all. As soon as they are able to toddle about, they are practically left to care for themselves. As a result, when their parents become old they show very little affection to them, letting them starve to death or even killing them outright.

The girls, with their mothers and sisters, slave in the village plantations. They maintain all the fences, bear every burden, and are knocked about by the men and boys. When the great chief Nouka became seriously ill, his people sacrificed three women for his recovery! How sad and degraded is the position of the woman where the teaching of Christ is unknown. It is the Christ of the Bible, His Spirit entering into humanity, that has lifted the woman and made her the helpmate and the friend of man, and not his toy or slave.

Leaving all consequences to the disposal of my Lord, I determined to make an unflinching stand against wife-beating and widow-strangling. I pleaded with all who were in power to unite and put down these shocking and disgraceful customs. At length ten chiefs entered into an agreement not to allow any more beating of wives or strangling of widows and to forbid all common labor on the Lord's Day. Alas, except for purposes of war or other wickedness, the influence of the chiefs on Tanna was comparatively small.

One chief boldly declared, "If we did not beat our women they would never work. They would not fear and obey us. But when we have beaten and killed and feasted on two or three, the rest are all very quiet and good for a long time to come!"

I tried to explain to him how cruel it was, besides the fact that the beatings sometimes made them unable to work, and that kindness would have a much better effect. He promptly assured me that Tannese women "could not understand kindness." For the sake of teaching by example, my Aneit-yumese teachers, their wives, and I used to go a mile or two inland on the principal pathway to cut firewood. Each of us men would carry a heavy load of wood while we gave only a small burden to each of the women. Meeting many Tannese men along the way, I explained to them that this was how Christians helped and treated their wives and sisters. Then our wives loved us and were strong to work at home. Since men were created stronger, they were intended to bear the heavier burdens.

During this time, several men, afraid or ashamed by day, came to me regularly by night for conversation and instruction. With the doors of the mission house secured and the windows covered so they could not be observed, they continued with me for many hours, asking questions about the "new" religion. The idea of a resurrection from the dead was that which most keenly interested the islanders.

The wife of a chief died, and he resolved to imitate a Christian burial. Having purchased white calico from a trader, he came to me for some tape. He wanted to dress the body as he had seen the body of my dear wife dressed, and to lay her in a similar grave. He declined my offer to attend the funeral and pray with them, as in that case many of the villagers would not attend. He wanted all the people to see and to hear this new kind of funeral; my friend Nowar the chief had promised to conduct a service and offer prayer to Jehovah. It moved me to many strange emotions—this Christian burial conducted by a lost soul and in the presence of lost souls, with an appeal to the True and Living God by one yet darkly groping among idols and superstitions!

On one occasion when a chief had died, the harbor people were all being assembled to strangle his widow. I ran to the village, and with much persuasion, saved her life. A few weeks later she gave birth to a young chieftain, to everyone's delight.

Soon after that, a sacred man was dying, and a crowd was awaiting the event in order to strangle his three wives. I spoke to them of the horrid wickedness of such conduct. I further reasoned with them that since some men had three wives, or a dozen wives, while many other men had none, this had caused great quarreling. I showed them how these widows being spared would make happy and helpful wives for other kind and loving husbands. I appealed to the chief and he replied, "Missi, strangling widows was introduced to Tanna from the island of Aneityum. Since the Aneityumese have given up the practice since they became worshipers of Jehovah, it is good that we should give it up on Tanna too." And so the three widows were spared.

Altogether, it was uphill, weary, and trying work. For one thing, the Tannese were terribly dishonest. Their skill in stealing was phenomenal! If an article fell or was seen on the floor, a Tannese man would neatly cover it with his foot while looking you in the face. Having fixed it by his toes or by grasping it with his big toe to hold it, he would then walk off with it. In this way a knife or pair of scissors would disappear. Another fellow would deftly place something out of sight among the whipcord braids of his hair. Another would conceal it under his naked arm while yet another would shamelessly lift what he coveted and openly carry it away.

One dark night I heard Tannese men among my fowls. Had I interfered they would have gloried in the chance to club or shoot me in the dark, for no one could say exactly who had done the deed. Several of the few goats that I kept for milk were also killed or driven away. Indeed, all the injury that was possible was done to me, short of taking my life, and that was not infrequently attempted.

One night all my cooking utensils were stolen. In consternation I appealed to the chief, telling him what had been done. He flew into a great rage and vowed vengeance on the thieves. He would compel them to return everything. Of course, nothing was returned; the thief could not be found! Unable to live without something in which to boil water, I offered a blanket to anyone who would bring back my kettle. Miaki himself, after much professed difficulty, returned it *minus* the lid.

One morning some Tannese rushed toward me in great excitement and cried, "Missi, Missi, there is a god, or a ship on fire, or something of fear, coming over the sea! We see no flames, but it smokes like a volcano. What is it? What is it?" One party after another followed in quick succession, shouting the same questions in great alarm.

"I cannot go at once," I replied. "I must dress first in my best clothes. It will likely be one of Queen Victoria's men-of-war coming to ask me if your conduct is good or bad, if you are stealing my property, or if you are threatening my life."

They pleaded with me to go and see it, but I made much fuss about dressing and getting ready

to meet the great chief on the vessel. The two principal chiefs now came running and asked, "Missi,
will it be a ship of war?"

"I think it will be," I called to them, "but I have
no time to speak to you now. I must get on my best
clothes!"

They said, "Missi, only tell us, will he ask you if
we have been stealing your things?"

"I expect he will."

"And will you tell him?" they asked.

I answered, "I must tell him the truth. If he
asks, I will tell him."

They then cried out, "Oh, Missi, don't tell him!
Everything will be brought back to you at once, and
no one will be allowed to steal from you again."

"Be quick! Everything must be returned before
he comes," I urged. "Away, away! And let me get
ready to meet the great chief on the man-of-war."

Before, no thief could be found, and no chief had
power to help me. Now, in an incredibly brief space
of time, one came running to the mission house
with a pot, another with a pan, another carrying a
blanket, others with knives, forks, plates, and all
sorts of stolen property. The chiefs called me to receive these things, but I declined, shouting, "Lay
them all down at the door. Get everything together
quickly. I have no time to speak with you!"

I washed and dressed slowly, enjoying mischie-
vously the magical effect of an approaching vessel
that might bring penalty to the thieves. At last the
chiefs, running in breathless haste, called out to
me, "Missi, Missi, do tell us, is the stolen property
all here?"

Of course I could not tell, but running out, I

looked on the miscellaneous heap of my belongings and said, "I don't see the lid of the kettle there yet!"

One chief said, "No, Missi, for it is on the other side of the island. But do not tell; I have sent for it, and it will be here tomorrow."

"I'm glad you have brought back so much," I answered, "and now, if you three chiefs, Nouka, Miaki, and Nowar, do not run away when the great chief comes, he will not likely punish you. But if you and your people run away, he will ask me why you are afraid and I will be forced to tell him! Keep near me and you are all safe. Only there must be no more stealing from me."

"We are in black fear," one replied, "but we will keep near you, and our bad conduct to you is done."

The charm and joy of that morning are fresh to me still, when the H.M.S. *Cordelia* steamed into our lovely harbor. The commander, having heard rumor of my dangers on Tanna, kindly came on shore as soon as the ship cast anchor. He was dressed in splendid uniform. Being a tall and handsome man, he and his attendants made a grand and imposing show.

Miaki spoke up, "Missi, this great chief whom Queen Victoria has sent to visit you in her man-of-war cannot go over the whole of this island so as to be seen by all our people. I wish you to ask him if he will stand by a tree and allow me to put a spear on the ground at his heel. We will make a nick in the spear at the level of his head, and the spear will be sent 'round the island to let all the people see how tall this great man is!"

They were delighted when the good captain agreed to their simple request. That spear was ex-

48

hibited to thousands, and the ship, her commander,
and officers were afterward spoken of all around
the island. The captain invited all the chiefs to go
on board and see the ship. He showed them two
shells to be discharged into the ocean. As the can-
nons roared and the shells fell far off into the water,
the terror of the islanders visibly increased. When
he sent a large ball crashing through a coconut
grove, breaking the trees like straws and cutting its
way clear and swift, they were quite dumbfounded
and pleaded to be again set safely on shore.

Fever and ague had attacked me fourteen times
severely, with slighter recurring attacks almost
continuously, after my first three months on the island. A chief advised me: "Missi, if you stay in this
house you will soon die! No Tannese sleeps so low
down as you do in this damp weather, or he too
would die. We sleep on the high ground, and the
trade wind keeps us well. You must go and sleep on
the hill, and then you will have better health."
I began to look for a suitable site. Behind my
present house rose a hill about three hundred feet
high or more, surrounded on all sides by a valley. It
was swept by the breezes of the trade winds, separated from the ocean only by a narrow neck of
land. I proceeded to buy up every claim to any portion of the hill, paying each publicly and in turn, so
that there might be no trouble later.
The fever smote me again more severely than
ever. With the help of my faithful Aneityumese
teacher, Abraham, and his wife, I made what felt
like my last effort to creep—I could not climb—up

the hill to get a breath of wholesome air. About two-thirds of the way up the hill, I became so faint that I concluded I was dying. Lying down on the ground, I said farewell to Abraham and to my mission work.

Abraham and his devoted wife, Nafatu, lifted me and carried me to the top of the hill. There they laid me on coconut leaves on the ground and erected over me a screen of the same. The two faithful friends gave me coconut juice to drink, fed me, and kept me alive. I do not know how long they personally attended me. Consciousness returned and the trade winds refreshed me day by day. The Tannese seemed to have given me up for dead, and providentially none of them came near us for many days. Amazingly, my strength returned, and I began planning my new house on the hill.

The peace party, my band of twenty harbor chiefs, kept all their tribes acting only on the defensive for a season. But the inland people murdered eight chiefs from distant villages while these eight were returning from a visit to the harbor. At the same time one of the peaceful inland chiefs was overthrown and murdered by his own men, along with his four wives and two children and his brother. Under a bloodthirsty new leader, that tribe declared war by shooting one of the harbor men and breaking down their fences and plantations. Once again the blood fiend was unleashed—the young men of Tanna being as eager to get up a battle as young men at home are to get up a dance.

The harbor people advised me to move a mile farther away from these warriors, but the inland tribes sent me word not to desert my house for they had no quarrel against me. Early the next morning

Abraham, another Aneityumese, and I started off to visit the inland party. We wanted to avert the impending war but without informing the harbor people. About four miles from our station we met our farthest inland friendly chief with all his fighting men, who reluctantly allowed us to pass. Praying to Jesus for guidance and protection, we pressed along the path through the thick bush another four miles. My two friends betrayed growing fear and insisted we walk in silence, though our hearts were going up to Jesus in prayer.

We passed many deserted villages and plantations, seeing no one. Unexpectedly, we stumbled upon the whole host assembled on a village common ground for a great feast, and every man rushed for his weapons. Keeping the teachers close beside me, I walked straight into the middle of them, unarmed of course, and cried as loudly as I possibly could in their own tongue, "My love to all you men of Tanna! Don't be afraid. I am your friend. I love you all and have come to tell you about Jehovah God and how to please Him!"

An old chief then took me by the hand, led me around the crowd, and said, "Sit down beside me here and talk with me. Before long they will not be afraid."

A few ran off to the bush in terror. Others appeared to be beside themselves with delight. They danced around us frantically, striking the ground and beating a canoe with their clubs, while shouting, "Missi is come! Missi is come!" The confusion grew wilder every moment. Men and boys rushed around, all painted and some with their hair stuck full of fantastic feathers. Women and children peeked through the bush, then instantly disappeared.

After spending about an hour conversing and answering questions, they apparently agreed to give up the war and allowed me to conduct worship among them. They presented me with coconuts, sugar cane, and two fowls, and I gave a red shirt to the principal chief and fishhooks and pieces of red calico among the rest. The leading men shook our hands graciously and invited us to come often, for after that visit they vowed they would harm no one connected with our mission.

The harbor people, having learned where we had gone, had concluded that we would all be killed and eaten. When we returned with presents of food, their astonishment was beyond measure. This had never happened on Tanna. The peace continued for more than four weeks, an uncommonly long truce. All hands were busy at work. Many yam plantations were completed, and all fences were repaired to excellent condition for the year.

The prejudices and persecutions of the idol-worshiping islanders were a sore enough trial, but worse was the wicked and contaminating influence of my fellow countrymen. A Captain Winchester, living with a native woman at the head of the bay as a trader, was angry at the present state of peace! Probably because there was not the usual demand for barter. He developed at once a wonderful interest in their affairs, presented all the chiefs with any amount of ammunition, and lent them a number of muskets, goading them into war.

Miaki the war chief had a young brother, Rarip, about eighteen years old. When the war began, Rarip came to live with me at the mission house.

52

Miaki forced him to join the fighting men, but he
escaped through the bush and returned to me.
Again the war chief came and forced dear young
Rarip to join the fight. I pleaded but could not prevent him. This time Miaki placed Rarip at his own
side. As they came within sight of the enemy a bul-
let pierced young Rarip's chest and he fell dead into
the arms of Miaki. The body was carried to Miaki's
village with much wailing, and a messenger ran to
tell me that Rarip was dead.

I ran to the village and found Rarip's body at the
center of a tragic ceremony. Sitting or lying on the
ground all around him were all the women and girls
of the village. They were tearing their hair out,
wounding themselves with split bamboos and broken
bottles, dashing themselves headlong to the ground,
painting all black their faces, breasts, and arms, and
wailing loudly! Men were knocking their heads
against the trees and gashing their bodies with
knives till they ran with streaks of blood. My heart
broke to see them and to think that they knew not
how to look to our dear Lord Jesus for consolation.

I returned to the mission house and brought
back a white sheet and some tape, in which the
body of dear Rarip was wrapped and prepared for
the grave. All seemed grateful for this mark of respect and agreed that Rarip should have a Christian burial under my direction. The men prepared
the grave in a spot selected near his house. I read
the Word of God, offered a prayer to Jehovah with
a psalm of praise, all amid a scene of weeping and
lamentation never to be forgotten. And the thought
burned through my very soul, *When will the
Tannese understand that what I am praying about*

is life and immortality in Jesus?

The war raged on and many more were killed. Miaki threatened vengeance on the trader: "You led us into this war. You deceived us. Rarip is dead and many others. Your life will go for his."

Captain Winchester, heartless as a dog so long as pigs and fowl were provided him—no matter the cost in others' lives—now trembled like a coward. He begged me to let him and his wife sleep at my house for safety, but I refused to allow my mission to be identified with his crimes in any way. His peril became so severe that by night he slept in his boat anchored out in the center of the bay, with his guns beside him, until finally a trading ship rescued him.

The war the captain had instigated lingered on for three months. Then, by a present given secretly to two leading chiefs, I brought it to a close.

All through the war I had gone to the fighting ground every Sunday and held worship among our harbor people. Hundreds assembled around me and listened respectfully, but they refused to quit fighting. When I decided to speak and pray with the inlanders also, the harbor folk opposed me, saying, "Missi, pray only for us! You must not pray with the enemy, lest He help them too." From then on I led worship at both camps. I taught them that Jehovah was angry at all such scenes and would not fight for either, that He commanded them to live at peace.

About this time, our Sunday gatherings at the mission numbered about forty. Only Nowar and three or four others seemed to love and serve Jesus. But even they were changeable and full of doubt.

4

In the Presence of My Enemies

Again the public assembly resolved that we should be killed. They hated Jehovah and the worship, they declared, for it made them afraid to do as they had always done. If I would give up visiting the villages, praying, and talking with them about Jehovah, they would like me to stay and trade with them. They liked the traders but hated the missionaries!

Within a few days islanders in large numbers were assembled at my house. One man furiously rushed on me with his axe, but a chief snatched a spade I had been using and defended me from instant death. Life in such circumstances led me to cling very near to the Lord Jesus. I never knew when or how an attack might be made. Yet with my trembling hand clasped in the hand once nailed on Calvary, and now swaying the scepter of the universe, calmness and peace abode in my soul.

The next day a wild chief followed me about with his loaded musket for four hours. Though it was often aimed at me, God restrained his hand. I spoke kindly to him and continued working as if he were not there. Looking up in unceasing prayer to our dear Lord Jesus, I left all in His hands and felt immortal till my work was done.

Namuri, one of my Aneityumese teachers, began working at our nearest village. Almost every morning he came and reported to me on the state of affairs. Without books or a school he instructed the villagers about God and conducted worship. His influence was increasing, and one morning a sacred man threw at him the *kawas,* or killing stone, a deadly weapon. It is a stone with a sharpened blade edge, eighteen to twenty inches long. They throw it from a great distance and with fatal precision. The teacher guarded his head and received a deep cut in his left hand, reserving his right hand to defend against the club that was certain to swiftly follow. The priest sprang upon him with his club and savage yells. The teacher evaded many blows, but also received many, and reached the mission station, bleeding, fainting, and pursued by howling murderers. I had been anxiously expecting him, and hearing the noise I ran out immediately.

Seeing me, he sank down by a tree and cried, "Missi, Missi, quick! Escape for your life! They are coming to kill you. They say they must kill us all today, and they have begun with me. They hate Jehovah and the worship!"

I rushed to his side and washed and dressed his wounds. God mysteriously kept the infuriated, watching Tannese at bay. They gradually disappeared into the bush, and we carried the dear teacher to my house. In three or four weeks he was able to walk about again. All about appeared friendly for a time, and he earnestly desired to return to his post. I pleaded with him to remain at the mission house, but he replied, "Missi, when I see them thirsting for my blood, I see myself when the missionary first came to my island. I wanted to murder him as they now desire to kill me. Had he stayed away because of danger, I would have remained lost. But he came and continued coming to teach us, till by God's grace I was changed to what I am. The same God that changed me can change these poor Tannese to love and serve Him. I cannot stay away from them. I will sleep at the mission house, but do all I can by day to bring them to Jesus."

For several weeks, things appeared most encouraging in his village work. But the villagers' declining fear of their priest fed the priest's jealousy, and one morning during worship, when the teacher knelt in prayer, the priest sprang upon him with his great club. All the people fled and left the unconscious teacher lying in his blood, thinking him dead. Coming to, he crawled to the mission station, reaching it at noon. I ran to meet him, but he fell near the teachers' house, saying, "Missi, I am dying. They will kill you also. Escape."

Trying to console him, I sat down beside him, dressing his wounds. He was rejoicing that he would soon be with Jesus in glory and was constantly praying for his persecutors, "Lord Jesus, forgive them for they do not know what they are doing. Do not take away your servants from Tanna! O God, bring all the Tannese to love and follow Jesus!"

After his death, I made a coffin for him and dug

his grave near the mission house. With prayers and many tears we consigned his remains to the dust in the certainty of a happy resurrection.

Immediately after this, a number of chiefs and their followers called on me at the mission house, professing great friendliness, and said, "Missi Turner gave our fathers calico, axes, and knives, and they became his friends. If you would give some of these things to the people they would be pleased and would stop fighting the worship."

I retorted, "How was it then, if they were pleased, that they persecuted Mr. Turner and Mr. Nisbet till they had to leave the island? Your conduct is deceitful. I will never reward you for your bad actions, much less for murder! I will give you no presents." They withdrew sullenly and seemed deeply offended.

———

There was great wonder on Tanna at this time when I began sinking a well. All our drinking water came from a boiling spring, and literally took days to cool down. Beyond that, no drinking water could be had for six or seven miles. Near the mission house I got a good supply of fresh water about twelve feet deep. However, even though it was fresh, the surface of the well rose and fell with every tide. This became the universal supply for us, the islanders all around the harbor, and for miles inland. Hundreds of Tannese from all parts of the island flocked to examine the greatest wonder they had ever seen—rain rising up out of the earth. Fortunately, the sinking of this well sparked no revolution.

For three months all our available time, with all
the help I could hire, was spent in erecting a building to serve for a church and school. As we were preparing the foundation, a huge and odd-looking
round stone was dug up. The Tannese stood aghast,
and their eldest chief said, "Missi, this stone was
either brought there by Karapanamun (the evil
spirit) or hid there by our great chief who is dead.
It is the Stone God to which our forefathers offered
human sacrifices. These holes held the blood of the
victim till drunk up by the spirit. The spirit of this
stone eats up men and women and drinks their
blood. We are in greatest fear!" A sacred man
claimed possession and was exceedingly desirous to
carry it off, but I managed to keep it from them.

The church-school was fifty feet long by twenty-
one and a half feet wide. The studs were three feet
apart and all fixed by tenon and mortise into upper
and lower wall plates. The beautiful roof of iron,
wood, and sugarcane leaf was supported by three
massive pillars of wood sunk deeply into the
ground. The floor was laid with white coral, broken
small, and covered with coconut leaf mats like
those the islanders sat on. I bought the heavy wood
on Aneityum for fifty pairs of native trousers, a gift
from my Bible class in Glasgow, all cut and sewn by
their own hands.

At first the Tannese opposed the building of a
church. They did not wish Jehovah to secure a
house on their island. On the opening day only
eleven people came, aside from the Aneityumese
teachers. But after the service that morning I visited ten villages and held worship in each.

The printing of my first book in Tannese was

thrilling for me. Though I had been given a printing press and type, I had never learned how to use it. Book printing turned out to be for me a much more difficult affair than building a house. By dogged perseverance I succeeded at last. My greatest difficulty was how to arrange the pages in the right order!

After many failures I folded a piece of paper into the number of leaves desired, cut the corners, folding them back, and numbered them as they would be when correctly placed in the book. Then I folded it all out flat again without cutting up the sheet. This pattern showed me how to arrange the pages in the frame for printing. Do you think me foolish when I confess that I shouted in ecstasy when the first sheet came from the press all correct? It was about one o'clock in the morning, and I pitched my hat into the air and danced like a schoolboy 'round and 'round the printing press till I began to think, *Am I losing my reason?* Would it not have been more like a missionary to have gone upon my knees, praising God for this first portion of His blessed Word ever printed in this new language? Friend, believe me, my reaction was as true worship as ever was David's dancing before the ark of God!

Dangers again darkened around me. While working near my house, Miaki the war chief, his brother, and a large party of armed men surrounded me. They all had muskets besides their own native weapons. They watched me for some time in silence and then every man leveled a musket straight at my head. Escape was impossible. Speech would only have increased my danger. My eyesight came and went for a few moments. I prayed to my Lord Jesus to either protect me or take me home. I tried to keep working at my task, as no one was near me. In that moment as never before the words came to me, "Whatever you ask in My name, I will do it," and I knew that I was safe. Backing away a little from their position, no words spoken, they took up the same positions a little farther off, and they seemed to be urging one another to fire the first shot. Once again my dear Lord restrained them, and they withdrew.

I had to move about more cautiously than ever. Some days I scarcely dared to appear outside the mission premises. I have always firmly believed that only when we use every lawful and possible means for preserving our lives can we expect God to protect us. For life is God's second greatest gift to us, His Son being the first.

Chief Nowar Noukamara was my best and most trusted friend. He was one of the nine or ten most favorable to the mission work, attending worship regularly, conducting it also in their own houses and villages. These professed Christ, though at times they were unstable. One or more of them often accompanied me on Sunday to the inland villages for worship and repeatedly protected me from personal injury. Nowar influenced the harbor chiefs and their people for eight or ten miles around to hold a great feast in favor of worship of Jehovah. It was the largest assembly I ever witnessed on the islands.

When all was ready, Nowar sent a party of chiefs to escort me and the Aneityumese teachers to the feast. Fourteen chiefs made speeches to the multitude: War should be given up on Tanna; no more people should be killed by *nahak*, for witchcraft and sorcery were lies; sacred men should no longer profess to make rain, famine, disease, or death; all people should adopt the worship of Jehovah as taught by the missionary and the Aneityumese; and all the banished tribes should be invited to their own lands to live in peace! There was not a single opposing voice. Doubtless they were in earnest, and had there been a leader to rule and mold them, their day would have dawned.

After these speeches an idolatrous ceremony began which horrified me. It was in connection with the pigs and fowl prepared for the feast. A great heap had been piled up for each tribe, and a handsome portion also set apart for the missionary and teachers.

The ceremony went like this as nearly as I could follow it: One hundred or so of the leading men marched into the large, cleared space in the center crowd. They faced each other in equal lines with a man at either end closing up the passage between. At the middle they stood eight or ten feet apart, gradually nearing like the sides of a triangle till they almost met at either end. Amid tremendous silence for a few moments, all stood hushed. Then every man kneeled on his right knee, extended his right hand and bent forward till his face nearly touched the ground. At this moment the man at the one end began muttering, his voice rising ever louder as he rose to his feet, and ended in a fearful yell as he stood erect. Next, the two long lines of men, all in a body, went through the same ritual, rising gradually to their feet with mutterings deepening into a howl, and swelling into a great yell as they stood erect. Finally, the man at the other end went through the same hideous forms. All this was repeated three times, each time with growing frenzy. And then, all standing on their feet, they united as with one voice in what sounded like music running madly up and down the scale, closing with a long, deep-toned, hollow howl as of souls in pain. Finally, the men all shook hands with each other with smiles of joy. Nowar and another chief spoke briefly and the food was divided and distributed, a leading man of each tribe standing by to receive his portion.

Nowar and Nerwangi spoke to me and the teachers, saying, "This feast is to move all the chiefs and people here to give up fighting, to become friends, and to worship your Jehovah God. We wish you to remain, and to teach us how to live right. As proof of our sincerity and of our love, we have prepared this pile of food for you."

In reply, I addressed the whole crowd, saying how pleased I was with their speeches and with the promises they all had made. I urged them to stick by these promises for their prosperity and for that of their children. I then walked to the very middle of the circle and laid down a bundle of calico, fish-hooks, knives, and other gifts. I asked the two chiefs to divide my presents among the assembled tribes along with a pile of the food presented to us, as a token of my love and friendship to them all.

They insisted I take their present of food, which forced me to explain my refusal. I again thanked them very warmly and explained that as they had in my presence given away all their food to Kara-panamun, the great evil spirit, my people and I could not eat it. Nowar and Nerwangi explained to the others how I wished all the food to be divided among the tribes to show my love, and they seemed highly satisfied.

Dances now began, paint, feathers, and ornaments adding to the wildness of the scene. The men danced in an inside ring, and the women in an outside ring, at a considerable distance from each other. Music was supplied by singing and clapping of hands. Their movements were in unison and highly intricate. After the dancing, all retired to the bush, and a kind of sham fight followed on the public ground. A host of painted warriors rushed in and took possession with songs and shouts. From the bush on the opposite side came women's chanting, louder and louder as they approached. Snatching flaming sticks from the fire, they rushed on the men, beating them and throwing burning pieces of wood among them till with deafening yells (amid shouts of laughter from the crowd) the women drove the men from the space and danced and sang a song of victory.

As they disbanded, the tribes freely mingled with each other. They stripped themselves of their fantastic dresses, their handsomely woven grass skirts, leaf skirts, and grass and leaf aprons. They gave away or exchanged all these, and their ornaments and bows and arrows. The generous gifts implied that they were a loving people, and so they were—for the feast.

Yet not a single feud was forgotten, and streams of blood and cries of hate would soon erase all traces of this day.

We now had six mission stations served by Aneityumese teachers, and as many more villages also
wanting a teacher. These teachers had all been cannibals once, but they proved to be a band of faithful
and devoted followers of Christ: Abraham, Kowari,
Nomuri, Nerwa, Lazarus, and Eoufati. Whenever
war broke out they all had to return to the mission
station, for they too had to bear persecution for
Jesus' sake.

The cruelty of the Tannese knew no bounds. One
woman pretended great friendship to the wife of
one of the teachers, even bringing dishes of food.
Having gained some trust, she caught a poisonous
little black fish and baked it into a meal for the un-
suspecting teacher's wife. Returning home she
boasted of her deed, and a friendly neighbor rushed
to warn the victim, but arrived to learn that the fatal meal had been eaten. The teacher's wife died
soon after in great agony—a martyr for Christ.

———

Before daybreak one morning, I heard shot after
shot quickly discharged in the harbor. One of the
teachers came running and cried out, "Missi, six or
seven men have been shot dead this morning for a
great feast. It is to reconcile tribes that have been
at war and to allow a banished tribe to return in
peace."

The leading men had agreed in council upon this
sacrifice, but the name of each victim was kept a
secret until the last moment. Before daylight the
sacred men allocated a murderer to the door of each
house where a victim slept. When the signal shot
was fired, the murderers rushed through their

doors, shooting and clubbing to death the doomed ones as they tried to escape. Their bodies were hung by the hands on a sacred tree as an offering to the gods. Taken down, they were carried ceremoniously onto the shore near my house.

I was told that my teachers and I were also designated victims for this same feast, and sure enough we spied a band of armed men coming toward us. The teachers, their wives, and I locked ourselves into the mission house. Cut off from all human hope we prayed to our dear Lord Jesus, either to protect us or take us to His glory. Till noon we heard them *tramp-tramping* around our house, whispering to each other. They knew we had a double-barreled fowling piece and a revolver, though they had never seen me use them. That may, under God, have held them back. But the thought of using weapons did not enter our souls even in that awful time. I had gone to save and not to destroy. It would be easier for me at any time to die than to kill one of them.

Toward sundown, constrained by the Invisible One, they withdrew from our mission house and left us once more in peace. They bore away the slain to be cooked and distributed among the tribes and eaten in their feast of reconciliation—a covenant sealed in blood, and soon to be buried in blood again!

For many days we took unusual care, for dark characters prowled about in the bush nearby, and we knew that our lives were the prize. We took what precautions we could, and God the Lord did the rest, or rather He did all—for His wisdom guided us, and His power baffled them.

5

Blinding Light, Deepening Shadows

During another war, I held a service in the village where a group of tribes assembled every morning. I declared that if they would follow Jehovah God, He would deliver them from all their enemies and lead them into a happy life. There were three witch doctors present—chiefs, heroes, experts in sorcery—claiming power over life and death, health and sickness, rain and drought. Hearing me, these three stood up and declared they did not believe in Jehovah. They did not need His help, for they had the power to kill me by *nahak*. If they could have a piece of leftover food from my plate, they could kill me.

A partially eaten piece of food was essential to their black art. To protect themselves from the witch doctors, people guarded banana peels, orange peels, and every scrap of uneaten food. Otherwise they could be killed by *nahak*. I asked a woman nearby if I could have some of the plums she was holding. "Take what you want," she said.

Calling out for the attention of the whole crowd,

I took a bite from three plums, and gave one to each of the three witch doctors. "You have seen me eat of this fruit," I shouted. "They have said they can kill me by *nahak*, but I challenge them to do it if they can, without arrow or spear, club or musket, for I deny that they have any power against me or against anyone by their sorcery alone."

When the challenge was accepted, the Tannese looked terror-stricken! They fled in panic, crying, "Missi Paton, run away! Alas, Missi!"

But I stayed to watch the *nahak* ceremony. Waving their arms and repeating magic spells, the witch doctors rolled up my plums in certain leaves of a sacred tree, shaping them like candles. Then they kindled a sacred fire near the root of the tree and continued their muttering, gradually burning a little more and a little more of the candle-shaped things, wheeling them round their heads, blowing on them, waving them in the air, and glancing wildly at me as if expecting my sudden destruction.

"Hurry up!" I urged them again and again. "Stir up your gods to help you! I am not killed yet. I am perfectly well!"

At last they stood up and spoke to me, "We must delay till we have called all our witch doctors. We will kill you, Missi, before your next Sunday comes. Let all watch, for you will soon die."

"Very good!" I replied. "I challenge all your priests to unite and kill me by *nahak*. If I return to your village healthy next Sunday, you will all admit that your gods have no power over me, and that I am protected by the True and Living Jehovah God!"

Every day that week they blew their conch shell trumpets. All the witch doctors were at work trying to kill me by their arts. Messengers arrived from all over the island, asking about my health, wondering if I was feeling sick. Great excitement rose among these idol worshipers.

Sunday dawned peacefully, and I returned to the village in more than my usual health and strength. Large numbers assembled, and when I appeared they looked at each other in terror, as if it could not really be me, still alive and well.

"My love to you all, my friends!" I saluted them. "I have come again to talk to you about Jehovah God and how to worship Him."

The three witch doctors admitted that they had tried to kill me by *nahak* but had failed. Why had they failed? I was also a sacred man. My God was stronger than theirs and had protected me.

"Truly, my Jehovah God is stronger than your gods. He has protected me and helped me. He is the only Living and True God, the only God that can hear or answer any prayer. Your gods cannot hear prayers, but my God can and will hear and answer you if you will give your hearts and lives to Him, and love and serve Him only. This is my God, and He is also your friend if you will hear and follow His voice."

Having said this, I sat down on the trunk of a fallen tree. "Come and sit down all around me, and I will talk to you about the love and mercy of my God, and teach you how to worship and please Him."

Two of the witch doctors sat down, and all the people gathered around and quietly sat down. I tried to present to them ideas of sin and of salvation through Jesus Christ. Meanwhile, the other sacred man, who was chief among the three, had gone off for his warrior's spear. He returned brandishing it in the air and aiming it at me. He was exceptionally tall and very strong.

"Of course he can kill me with his spear," I said, "but he pledged to kill me by *nahak*, and promised not to use any weapons. If you let him kill me now, you will kill your friend, one who lives among you and only tries to do you good, as you all know so well. If you kill me in this way, my God will be angry and will punish you."

I remained calmly seated in the middle of the crowd while the great chief leaped about in rage, scolding everyone for listening to me. The other witch doctors, however, took my side. Many of the people were friendly to me and stood closely packed around me, so he did not throw his spear. To avoid bloodshed, I offered to leave.

For weeks after that, wherever I went, the angry chief would suddenly appear on the path behind me, holding in his right hand that same Goliath spear. God alone kept him from throwing it. I kept at my work, as if no enemy were there, leaving the results in the hands of Jesus.

If not truly converted, the two other priests were fast friends of mine from that day. They received an Aneityumese teacher in their village, protecting and showing kindness to him. A few from that village began to pray to Jehovah in their houses, offering a kind of family worship. They accompanied me when I visited in their district.

In September 1860, I welcomed two new missionaries to Tanna. They were the Rev. S. F. Johnston and his wife, both from Nova Scotia. Having visited the whole group of islands, they had chosen Tanna. During the rainy season and until they had acquired a little of the language, I gladly received them as my guests. Each day I gave them fourteen Tannese words to memorize and conversed with them, using the words already acquired. They made very rapid progress and were of almost immediate service in the mission work.

———

Sandalwood traders murdered many of the islanders when robbing them of their wood, and the islanders killed many of the traders and their servants in revenge. Unwilling to watch as their children's only food was stolen, natives interfered and were shot down without mercy. Vengeance called for the life of every white man.

The traders' infernal spirit knew no limits. One morning three or four vessels entered our harbor and cast anchor. The captains called on me and one exclaimed with delight, "We know how to bring down your proud Tannese now! We'll humble them before you! Four young men with measles have been landed at different ports, and these will soon thin their ranks. Our watchword is: Sweep these creatures away and let white men occupy the soil!"

The measles spread fearfully, accompanied by sore throat and diarrhea. In some villages all were stricken, leaving none to give food or water to the rest. Thirteen of my own mission party died of this disease. So terror-stricken were the few who survived that when the little mission schooner *John*

Knox returned to Tanna, they all packed up and returned to their own Aneityum, except dear old Abraham. He said, "Missi, I remain with you of my own free choice, and with all my heart. We will live and die together in the work of the Lord. I will never leave you while you are spared on Tanna." Thereafter, Abraham was my dear companion and constant friend, and my fellow sufferer in all that remains to be told of our work on Tanna.

Mr. Johnston and his wife assisted me in every way to alleviate the dread sufferings of the islanders. We carried medicine, food, and even water to the surrounding villages every day, few being able to render us much assistance. Nearly all who took our medicine and followed our instructions recovered, but vast numbers would not listen to counsel and rushed into experiments which made the attack fatal all around. They would plunge into the sea for relief and find in it almost instant death. Others would dig a hole in the earth, the length of the body and two feet deep. There they would lay themselves down, the cold earth soothing to their fevered skins. When the earth around them grew heated, they got friends to dig a few inches deeper, again and again, seeking a cooler and cooler couch. In this ghastly effort many of them died, literally in their own graves, and were buried where they lay.

Though we did everything in our power to relieve and save them, the islanders associated us with the white men who had so dreadfully afflicted them. Their blind thirst for revenge did not draw fine distinctions between the traders and the missionaries. All were whites—that was enough.

The first of January, 1861, was a New Year's Day

ever to be remembered. Mr. and Mrs. Johnston, Abraham, and I spent nearly the whole time in a solemn, yet happy festival. We consecrated our lives and our all to the Lord Jesus, giving ourselves away to His blessed service for the conversion of the lost in these islands. After evening family worship, Mr. and Mrs. Johnston left my room to go to their own house, only some ten feet distant. He returned to inform me that there were two men at the window, armed with huge clubs, and having black painted faces. Going out to them and asking them what they wanted, they replied, "Medicine for a sick boy."

After I got them the medicine both men raised their clubs to strike me, but quick as lightning my two dogs sprang at their faces and baffled their blows. I sent both dogs furiously upon them and the two fled. I shouted after them, "Remember, Jehovah God sees you and will punish you for trying to murder His servants!"

Now accustomed to such scenes, I slept soundly, but Mr. Johnston could not sleep at all. Next morning he told me, "I can only keep saying to myself, 'Already on the verge of Eternity! How have I spent my time? What good have I done? What zeal for souls have I shown?' Scarcely entered on the work of my life, and so near death! O my friend, I never realized what death means, till last night!" His pallor and distress continued for several days. After that, though he was energetic and pleasant, I never saw him smile again.

Mr. Johnston scarcely ever slept after that, and during the night of the sixteenth he sent for my bottle of laudanum. Under a severe attack from ague and fever, I could not go to him but sent the bottle. He took a dose for himself and gave one also to his wife, as she too suffered from sleeplessness. This he repeated three nights in succession, and both of them obtained a long, sound, and refreshing sleep. He came to my bedside and said, "I have had such a blessed sleep and feel so refreshed! What kindness in God to provide such remedies for suffering humans!"

At midday his dear wife came to me, crying, "Mr. Johnston has fallen asleep so deeply that I cannot wake him."

My fever had reached the worst stage, but I had to struggle to my feet and get to his bedside. I found him in a state of coma with his teeth fixed in tetanus. With great difficulty we succeeded in slightly rousing him. With a knife, spoon, and pieces of wood, we forced his teeth open, so as to administer an emetic with good effects. For twelve hours we had to keep him awake by repeated cold dashes in his face, by ammonia, and by vigorously moving him about. He then began to speak freely, and the next day he rose and walked about a little. The following two days he was sometimes better and sometimes worse. We kept him up till the morning of the twenty-first. Then he fell into a state of coma from which we could not rouse him. At two o'clock in the afternoon he fell asleep, another martyr for the testimony of Jesus in those dark and trying islands, leaving his young wife in indescribable sorrow.

Having dug his grave, we two alone at sunset laid him to rest beside my own dear wife and child, close by the mission house. Mrs. Johnston recovered gradually, returning at the first opportunity to Aneityum. After teaching for three years at the girls' school there, she married my dear friend, Joseph Copeland, and worked with him the rest of her life on the island of Fotuna.

Another tragedy followed with much of the light of heaven in its shadows. Kowia was a Tannese chief of the highest rank. Going to Aneityum as a youth, he had become a true Christian there. He married a Christian Aneityumese woman with whom he lived very happily, and they had two beautiful children. Sometime before the measles reached our island he returned with his family to live with me as a teacher and to forward God's work on Tanna. His own people tried everything to induce him to leave me and renounce the worship of Jehovah—every honor and bribe in their power. Failing in all their attempts, they threatened to take away all his lands and deprive him of his chieftainship. "Take all!" he said. "I shall still stand by Missi and the worship of Jehovah."

From threats they switched to galling insults, and he bore all patiently for Jesus' sake. But one day a party of his people came and sold him some fowl. After they had been paid for, an impudent fellow took them back and offered to sell them again to me. Kowia shouted, "Don't purchase them, Missi. I have just bought them for you!"

The seller began to mock him, and Kowia rose like a lion awaking out of sleep, and with flashing eyes exclaimed, "Missi, they think that because I am now a Christian I have become a coward! I will show them that I am no coward, that I am still their chief, and that Christianity does not take away from us but rather gives courage."

Springing at one man, he wrenched the mighty club from his hands. "Come, any of you," he cried, "come all against your chief! My Jehovah God makes my heart and arms strong. He will help me in this battle as He helps me in other things, for He inspires me to show you that Christians are not cowards, though they are men of peace." All fled as he approached them, and he shouted, "Where are the cowards now?" Then he handed back the club to its owner. After this they left him in peace.

At the time of Mr. Johnston's death the ague and fever had reduced me to such weakness that I had become insensible, while Abraham and Kowia alone attended me. Returning to consciousness, I heard as in a dream Kowia lamenting over me and pleading with God that I might recover so as to speak with him before he himself died. I heard him say, "Missi, all our Aneityumese are sick. Missi Johnston is dead. You are very sick, and I am weak and dying. Alas, when I am dead, who will climb the trees and get you a coconut to drink? Who will bathe your lips and brow?" Here he broke down into deep and long weeping.

I began under the breath of God's blessing to revive. A few days later Kowia came to me again, and rousing me out of sleep, said, "Missi, I am very weak. I am dying. I come to bid you farewell and go away to die. I am nearing death now, and I will soon see Jesus. Since you became ill my dear wife and children are dead and buried. If I remain on the hill and die here at the mission house, there are none left to help Abraham carry me down to the grave where my wife and children are laid. I wish to lie beside them so that we may rise together in the Great Day when Jesus comes for us. I am happy, looking to Jesus! Only one thing deeply grieves me now: I fear God is taking us all away from Tanna and will leave my poor people in the darkness as before, for they hate Jesus and the worship of Jehovah. O Missi, pray for them, and pray for me once more before I go!"

He knelt down at my side, and we prayed for each other and for Tanna. With many tears he dragged himself away. My heartstrings seemed all tied round that noble simple soul and felt like they were breaking one by one as he left me there on my bed of fever. Abraham helped him, tottering to the place of graves. There he lay down, and immediately gave up the ghost and slept in Jesus. Faithful Abraham buried Kowia beside his wife and children. So died a cannibal chief, but by the grace of God and the love of Jesus, changed, transfigured into a character of light and beauty.

This terrible plague of measles swept away a third of the population of Tanna, and in certain localities more than a third. Even a larger proportion died on Aniwa, the scene of my future sorrow but greater triumphs.

The traders, in order to divert attention from themselves, stirred the islanders with the wild idea that the missionaries and the worship of Jehovah had brought all this sickness. They said that our lives should be taken in revenge. Some captains made a pretense of refusing to trade with the islanders as long as I was permitted to live on the island.

Hurricane and tempest also fought against us at that time. Twice in March of 1861 we had destructive storms. They tore up and smashed breadfruit, chestnut, coconut, and all kinds of fruit trees. Trees of forty years' growth were broken like straws or lifted by the roots and blown away. Waves rolled far inland, causing terrible destruction. Had not the merciful Lord left one bedroom at my station partly livable, I do not know what I would have done. Men of fifty years declared that never had such a tempest shaken their island. Canoes were shattered on the coral rocks, and villages were left with nothing but ruins to mark where they had been. Though rain poured in torrents, I had to keep near my fallen house for hours and hours to prevent the islanders from carrying away everything I had in this world.

———

A teacher's child was the first to be baptized on Tanna. About fifty persons had come, including Miaki the war chief. Alas, that child died in the plague of measles, and of course the worship was blamed. Deaths, hurricanes, all seemed to be turned against us.

We were blamed for the storms and also for the death of Chief Miaki's infant son. For four days they surrounded our diminished premises. We locked ourselves up in that single bedroom, and armed men kept prowling about to take our lives. They killed our fowl. They cut down and destroyed all our remaining bananas. They killed some of the few goats—our sole source of milk. We were helpless and kept breathing out our souls in prayer. God preserved us, but what a trying time!

The horror grew when, soon after, the harbor people killed four men for feasting. Within a few months, thirteen or fourteen persons had been killed and eaten. They sent two dead bodies to the nearest village (where we still conducted worship every Sunday we dared go), but our people refused to receive them, saying, "Now we know that it is wrong to kill and eat our fellow men." A chief visiting from another village eagerly received them and carried them off to a great feast he was preparing.

The month of May brought further tragedy in the martyrdom of the Gordons on nearby Erromanga. On the twentieth of May, 1861, Rev. G. N. Gordon was roofing his printing office and had sent his helpers to each bring a load of long grass to finish the thatching. Meantime, a party of Erromangans had been watching him and knew he was now alone. They sent two of their men to ask the missionary for calico. On a piece of wood he wrote a note to Mrs. Gordon to give them two yards each. They asked him to go with them to the mission house for medicine needed for a sick boy. Gordon requested the Erromangans to lead, but they insisted on his going in front of them. In crossing a small stream his foot slipped. A blow was aimed at him with a tomahawk which he caught with his hand. The other man struck, but Gordon caught that weapon in his hand too. One of the tomahawks was wrenched from his grasp, and the next moment a blow was laid to his spine and a second on the neck. The others then rushed from their ambush and slashed him to pieces. They began dancing around him with frantic shouting. Mrs. Gordon heard the noise and came out and stood in front of the mission house, wondering what had happened. One of the party had run toward the house the moment Mr.

Gordon fell and now approached her. A merciful clump of trees hid from her eyes all that had occurred, and she asked, "What is causing the noise?"

"Oh, nothing," she was told.

Turning around, she asked, "Where are the boys?" The Erromangan sank his tomahawk into her back and with another blow struck her head.

Loving in their lives, and in their deaths scarcely divided, the Gordons' spirits entered glory together, to be welcomed by Williams and Harris, martyrs on that same island.

Immediately a trader brought a party of Erromangans to Tanna by night. They assembled our harbor chiefs and people and urged them to kill us and the Mathiesons and the teachers, or allow *them* to do so as they had killed the Gordons. Then they proposed to go to Aneityum and kill the missionaries there, and so they would sweep away the worship and the servants of Jehovah from their islands. Our chiefs refused, restrained by the Merciful One, and the Erromangans returned to their own island in a sulky mood.

As if the Tannese wished to reserve our murder and plunder for themselves, they thronged our house the next day, some from inland and others from Mr. Mathieson's area. They loudly praised the Erromangans again and again, "The men of Erromanga killed Missi Williams long ago. We killed the Samoan Christian teachers. We fought Missi Turner and Missi Nisbet and drove them from our island. We killed the Aneityumese teachers on Aniwa and one of Missi Paton's teachers too. We killed several white men and no man-of-war punished us. Let us talk this over about killing Missi Paton and the Aneityumese till we see if a man-of-war comes to punish the Erromangans. If not, let us unite! Let us kill these missionaries! Let us drive the worship of Jehovah from our land!"

I stood among them and protested, "God will yet punish the Erromangans for such wicked deeds. God has heard all your bad talk and will punish it in His own time and way."

But they shouted me down, crying in unison, "Our love to the Erromangans! Our love to the Erromangans!"

After I left, Abraham heard them say, "Miaki the harbor chief is lazy. Let us meet in every village. Let us all agree to kill Missi and the Aneityumese for the first of our chiefs that died from measles."

Abraham and I were thrown much into each other's company, and he stood by me in every danger. We conducted family prayers alternately in Tannese, the only language we shared. That evening he prayed, "O Lord, our heavenly Father, they have murdered your servants on Erromanga. They have banished the Aneityumese from dark Tanna. And now they want to kill Missi Paton and me! Our great King, protect us, and make their hearts soft and sweet to your worship. Or, if they are permitted to kill us, do not hate us, but wash us in the blood of your dear Son, Jesus Christ. Through Him forgive us our sins and take us to heaven—that good place where Missi Gordon the man and Missi Gordon the woman and all your dear servants now are singing your praise and seeing your face. Our Lord, our hearts are pained, and we weep over the death of your dear servants, but make our hearts strong for your cause. Take away all our fears. Make us two and all your servants strong for you and your worship. And if they kill us two, let us die together in your good work, like your servants Missi Gordon the man and Missi Gordon the woman."

In this manner his great soul poured itself out to God, and my heart melted within me as it had never done under any prayer from the lips of my countrymen!

Superstition ran deep. One morning two inland chiefs came running to the mission house, breathless, and covered with perspiration. One of them held up a handful of half-rotten tracts, crying, "Missi, is this a part of God's Word, the sacred Book of Jehovah? Or is it the work, the words, the book of man?"

Examining them, I replied, "These are the work, the words, and the book of man, not of Jehovah."

"Missi, are you certain it is not the Word of Jehovah?"

"Yes, but it is man's work and man's book."

He continued then, "Missi, some years ago Kaipai, a sacred Tannese chief, visited Aneityum, and Missi Geddie gave him these books. When he showed them to his people, they were all afraid for they thought they were the sacred Book of Jehovah. They solemnly agreed to bury them. Yesterday someone accidentally dug them up. Our inland people said that our dead chief made Jehovah angry by burying part of His Word, and that Jehovah caused the chief's death and the plague of measles. They were now assembled to kill the dead chief's son and daughter in revenge! I persuaded them to send these books to find out from you if this is part of Jehovah's Book, and if the burying of it caused all these diseases and deaths."

I assured him that these books never caused either sickness or death to anyone, and that none of us can cause sickness or death by sorcery, that burying these tracts did not make Jehovah angry, nor cause evil to any creature. "You yourselves know the very ships that brought the measles and caused the deaths."

"Missi," the inland chief declared, "I am quite satisfied. No person shall be put to death over these books now."

They went off but immediately returned, saying, "Missi, have you any books like these to show us? And will you show us the sacred Book of Jehovah beside them?"

I showed them a Bible and then a handful of tracts with pictures like those they had brought. I offered them the Bible and tracts to show their people. The tracts they received, but the Bible they refused to touch. The tracts satisfied their people and prevented bloodshed.

Revenge for the murder of four men killed to accompany Chief Miaki's child to the next world threatened to start another war. The chiefs for eight miles around met and agreed that as they were all weak for war, owing to the measles and the shortage of food from the hurricanes, they should delay till they all grew stronger.

Miaki, however, urged an inland tribe to shoot Chief Nowar, Abraham, and me. Nowar pleaded with us to take him and flee to Aneityum—next to impossible even with a canoe. That night they tried to break into my house. My faithful dog gave a sharp bark and woke me. At other times, she leapt up and pulled at my clothes till I awoke. Then she would turn her head to indicate where the danger lay.

They became more peaceful toward me for a season because of my fishing net. Seeing that they had so little food after the hurricane, I hired an inland tribe to make a net forty feet long and very wide. Strange to say, the inland people who live far from the sea make the best fishing materials, which they sell to the harbor people for axes, knives, and blankets obtained by trading from passing ships. The inland women and girls manufactured for me this huge fishing net. The cord was twisted from the fiber of a certain tree bark and prepared with immense toil and care. I lent the net about three days to each village around and near the harbor. The harbor yielded them much wholesome food in place of what the hurricane had destroyed.

The friendly feeling grew on every side. For payment, the islanders prepared an excellent foundation for a new church. All the fences were mended, and the mission premises began to look nice once more. My work became encouraging, and I had many opportunities of talking with them about worship and Jehovah.

All this displeased Miaki so that one of his men kindled a fire under the veranda of my house. Our watch had to be unrelenting. Miaki's cousin sold me a poisonous fish, but Nowar saw it in time and warned me. Miaki then threatened to shoot any of the inland people who came to work for me or receive instruction from me. Larger numbers came than before, but they came fully armed! For some time Nouka and nine other chiefs attended worship regularly at the mission house—on Sundays and on Wednesday afternoons. In all, about sixty persons regularly attended services at this time. Yet one evening, when we were feeling more consoled and hopeful than ever before, a musket was discharged at my very door. We were still in the midst of death.

As my work became more encouraging, I urgently applied to the missionaries on Aneityum for more teachers, but none could be found willing to return to Tanna. I shouldn't have wondered why; smaller perils deter God's people at home from many a call of duty.

In the mission school I offered as a prize a red shirt for the first chief who knew the whole alphabet. It was won by a chief who had been a terror to the whole community. When teaching the ABCs to others he proceeded like this, "A is a man's legs with the body cut off. B is like two eyes. C is a three-quarter moon. D is like one eye. E is a man with one club under his feet and another over his head. F is a man with a large club and a smaller one" and so on. Then he would say, "Remember these things. You will soon get hold of the letters and be able to read. I have taught my little child, who can scarcely walk, the names of all the letters. They are not hard to hold but soft and easy. You will soon learn to read the book if you try it with all your heart!"

One day the *John Knox* came into the harbor with two great ships of fire, men-of-war, behind her. Those who were most friendly flocked to us from all parts of the island. They clamored to have Miaki and others of our enemies punished by the men-of-war. Then they would feel strong to speak in our defense and lead the Tannese to worship Jehovah.

After inquiring into everything, the commodore urged me to leave at once and kindly offered to take me to Aneityum or even New Zealand. I hesitated to leave my dear, lost Tannese, knowing that both stations would be instantly broken up, that all the influence gained would be thrown away. The church would lose all that had been expended. Above all, those friendly to us would be left to persecution and destruction. For a long time I had seldom taken off my clothes at night, needing to be ready for attack at a moment's notice. Yet while hope burned in my soul I could not withdraw, so I resolved to risk all with my dear Lord Jesus and remain at my post.

At my request the officers met with all the leaders who could be assembled. At length old Nouka spoke out for all, "The traders tell us that the worship causes all our sickness and death. They will not trade with us, nor sell us tobacco, pipes, powder, balls, caps, and muskets till we kill our Missi like the Erromangans did. After that they will send a trader to live among us and give us plenty of all these things. We love Missi. But when the traders tell us that the worship makes us sick, and when they bribe us with tobacco and powder to kill him or drive him away, some believe them, and our hearts turn against Missi. Let Missi stay here, and we will try to do good to him, but you must tell Queen 'Toria of her people's bad treatment of us. She must stop her traders from killing us with their measles and from telling us lies about Missi! If they come to us and talk as before, our hearts will grow very dark and may again lead us to bad conduct to Missi."

The men-of-war inflicted no punishment at Erromanga, and the Tannese were soon as bold and wicked as ever. Thus light and shadow pursued each other, the light brightening for a moment, but upon the whole the shadows deepening.

6

The Final War

A time of great excitement was stirring among the islanders. War, war, nothing but war was spoken of! Preparations were under way in all the villages far and near. Fear showed on every face, and armed bands watched each other, uncertain where the war would begin or by whom. All work was suspended. Again we found ourselves to be the center of conflict: one party set on killing us or driving us away from Tanna, the other wishing to keep us. The harbor chiefs, Miaki and Nouka, said, "If you will keep Missi and his worship, take him with you to your own land. We will not have him live near the harbor."

The great inland chief, Ian, rose in anger and said, "On whose land does the Missi live? yours or ours? Who fights against the worship and good, who are the thieves and murderers; who tells the lies— you or us? We wish peace, but you want war. We like Missi and the worship. It is our land where he now lives. He bought it from you, but our fathers sold it to Missi Turner long ago. The land was not yours to sell, but ours. After your fathers stole it from us long ago by war, we would not have asked it back.

But now you ask us to take Missi Paton away. We will defend him on it, and he will teach us."

Meeting after meeting broke into fiery speeches and separated with many threats.

Miaki and his party brought a large present of food to Ian and his men as a peace offering. Ian accepted it, and the next day he brought Miaki a return present and said, "You know that Missi lives on our land. Take our present, friends, and let him live quietly and teach us all. We will defend Missi."

Miaki accepted the token and gave promises of peace for the future. Ian then came to the hilltop near our house. Standing by the public path, he cried aloud, "Abraham, tell Missi that you and he now live on our land. This path is the mark between Miaki and us. We have today bought back the land of our fathers by a great price to prevent war. Take of our breadfruits and also of our coconuts, as much as you need. You are our friends, and we will protect you and the worship.

For some time after this things moved quietly. An inland war, however, had been going on for months. As many as ten men, people said, were killed in one day and feasted on by the opposing warriors.

Ever full of revenge, Nouka and Miaki declared publicly that they were now going to kill Ian by *nahak*, more feared by the Tannese than the battlefield. Ian soon became very sick. I did all that could be done, but all thought him to be dying. Though he had symptoms of poisoning, everyone suspected the sorcery. Ian's people were angry at me for not consenting before to shooting Miaki. Ian's brother came for me to go and see Ian. Upon reaching his village, I saw many people about and feared I had been led into a snare, but I entered his house at once to talk and pray with him. After prayer I discovered that I was alone with him. In fact, all the people had left the village. I knew this meant something was amiss. Ian said, "Come near me, and sit by my bedside to talk with me, Missi."

I did so. While I was speaking he lay as if lost in silent meditation. Suddenly he drew a large butcher-like knife from the sugarcane thatch by his bed. Feeling the edge of it with his other hand, he pointed it to within a few inches of my heart and held it quivering there. I dared neither move nor speak, but silently prayed. There passed a few moments of awful suspense. My sight went and came. Not a word had been spoken. Then Ian wheeled the knife around, thrust it into the sugarcane leaf, and cried to me, "Go, go quickly!"

The next moment I was on the road. Not a living soul was to be seen in the village. I understood then that Ian had agreed to kill me, and all had withdrawn so as not to witness it. When the man-of-war came to inquire about me, Ian would already be dead, and no punishment could overtake the murderer. I walked quietly until I was outside the village in case someone hiding in a house might observe me. Then I ran for my life, a weary four miles, till I reached the mission house. Poor Ian died soon after, and his people strangled one of his wives and hanged another and took the three bodies out in a canoe together and sank them in the sea.

Miaki was jubilant over having killed his enemy by *nahak*. The inland people now assembled in the thousands to help avenge Ian's death by killing

Miaki and Nouka. On the eighteenth of January, 1862, the war began. Musket after musket discharged near us. The bush rang with the yell of their unforgettable war cry. It came nearer and nearer, for Miaki was retreating and taking shelter with his people behind our house. We were placed in the heart of the danger; the balls flew thick all around us. In the afternoon Ian's brother and his party retired.

Miaki sent messengers and presents to the Inikahimini and Kaserumini districts to assemble all their people and help him fight Missi and the Tannese who were friends of the worship. He said, "Let us cook Missi's body and Abraham's, and distribute them to every village on this side of the island." Yet all the while, Miaki assured me he had sent a friendly message.

The war went on, and Nowar defended us till he had a spear broken in his right knee. The enemy would have carried him off to feast on his body, but his young men, wildly shouting his name and their battle cry, rushed in and carried their wounded chief home in triumph.

The inland people now discharged muskets at my house and beat against the walls with their clubs. They smashed in the door and window of our storeroom, broke open boxes and casks, tore my books to pieces, and carried off my boat, mast, oars, and sails. They broke into Abraham's house and looted it as well. Then they made a rush at my bedroom where we had locked ourselves. Firing muskets and yelling, they tried to break in. A chief, professing to be sorry for us, called me to the window;

seeing me he threw a tomahawk, crying, "Come on, let's kill him now!"

"My Jehovah God will punish you," I replied. "A man-of-war will come and punish you, if you kill Abraham, his wife, or me."

"It's all lies about a man-of-war!" he retorted. "They did not punish the Erromangans. They are afraid of us. Come on, let's kill him!"

He raised a tomahawk to strike my forehead, and many muskets were raised to shoot, so I raised a revolver in my right hand and pointed it at them. Rev. Joseph Copeland had left it with me on a former visit. I did not want it, but he insisted on leaving it, saying that the very knowledge that I owned such a weapon might save my life. Now it did so. Though it was harmless, they fell back quickly, crying, "Missi has a short musket! He will shoot you all!"

After lying flat on the ground for a little, they got up and ran to the nearest cover, where they stayed. In the evening, after they left, I went to Miaki and Nouka. They professed great sorrow at what had taken place and said they had given our attackers a present of food not to harm us. Nowar told us, however, that Miaki and Nouka had hired them to return and kill us the next morning.

Miaki said with a sneer, "Missi, where was Jehovah today? It's all lies about Jehovah. They will come and kill you, Abraham, and his wife, and cut your bodies into pieces to be cooked and eaten in every village on Tanna."

"Surely Jehovah did protect us," I replied, "or we would not be here!"

I sent Abraham to consult with Nowar, who had

defended us until he was disabled by the spear in his knee. Nowar sent Abraham back in a canoe, advising me to take some of my goods to his house by night, and he would try to protect us. Enemies waited on every hand to cut off our flight. Abraham, his wife, and I prayed anxiously till the morning light. Miaki, the false and cruel, came to assure us that no one would come that day.

As daylight came, Miaki himself stood and blew a great conch shell near our house. I ran out to see why this trumpet shell had been blown and found it was the signal for a great company of howling, armed men to rush down the hill on the other side of the bay and make straight for the mission house. We had not a moment to lose. To remain was certain death for us all, including Matthew, a teacher newly arrived.

Though I am by conviction a strong Calvinist, I am no fatalist. Escape was now the only path of duty. I called the teachers, locked the door, and made quickly for Nowar's village. There was not a moment left to carry anything with us except my Bible, the few translations which I had made into Tannese, and a light pair of blankets. The loss was bitter for me: all my deceased wife's clothing, her piano, silver, cutlery, and books, besides all my personal belongings, had to be left behind.

The traders bought all the stolen property for tobacco, powder, balls, caps, and shot. One trader gathered a number of my books in a sadly torn condition and took them to Aneityum, demanding payment from my colleague for his trouble.

We could not take the usual path along the beach, so we entered the bush in the hope of getting away unobserved. Suddenly a cousin of Miaki sprang from behind a breadfruit tree, swinging his tomahawk and aiming it at my brow. I spoke to him in a firm, bold voice, "If you dare to strike me, Jehovah God will punish you. He is here to defend me now!"

Trembling, the man looked all around as if to see the God who was my defender, and the tomahawk gradually lowered to his side. Keeping my eyes fixed on him, I gradually moved backward in the track taken by the teachers, and God mercifully restrained him from following me.

The people in Nowar's village were terror-stricken, for an army was approaching. I urged them to cut down trees and blockade the path. They worked vigorously at this till they saw the overwhelming size of the attacking army. The men threw away their weapons and cast themselves headlong on the ground or knocked themselves against the trees, as if to court death before it came. Mothers snatched up little children and ran to hide in the bush. Others carried their children as far as they could into the sea, holding their children's heads above water.

Nowar, lame from his wounded knee, got a canoe turned upside down and sat upon it, where he could see the whole advancing multitude. He said, "Missi, sit down beside me, and pray to our Jehovah God. If He does not send deliverance now, we are all dead men. They will kill us all on your account. Pray, and I will watch."

When the warriors got within three hundred yards, at the foot of a hill leading up to the village, Nowar touched my knee, saying, "Missi, Jehovah is hearing! They are all standing still."

If they had come they would have met no opposition because the people were scattered in terror. Gazing shoreward and around the harbor, as far as we could see was a dense host of warriors, but all were standing still. We saw a messenger running along their front, delivering news as he passed. To our amazement the army began to turn. They marched back in silence and entered the far-off bush at the head of the harbor. Nowar and his people shouted ecstatically, "Jehovah has heard Missi's prayer! Jehovah has protected us and turned them away."

We learned that the leaders of the army all assembled and had a great debate. Nouka and Miaki advised them to fight Manuman and his people first, saying, "Manuman is a friend of Missi and of the worship. He also sent the hurricane to destroy us. They have plenty of yams and pigs. Let us fight and plunder them. When they are out of the way, we will be strong to destroy Missi and the worship."

So the whole mass went and attacked Manuman's first village. The inhabitants fled, and all the sick, the feeble, and the children who fell into their hands were reported to be murdered, cooked, and eaten. Led on by Miaki, they plundered and burned seven villages.

About midday Nouka and Miaki sent their cousin Jonas, who had always been friendly to me, to say I could return to my house in safety. All their men were carrying the war inland. That night, Abraham ventured near the mission house twice, but was stopped both times. Seeing that I was not there, Nouka ordered, "Don't kill Abraham now!

•

Wait till Missi comes." We gave up all hope of recovering anything from the house.

I lay on the ground all night, concealed in an outhouse of Nowar's, but it was a sleepless and anxious night, not only to me and the Aneityumese but also to Nowar and his people. Messages came to Nowar, threatening to kill him and his people for protecting me. Next day the attack was renewed in my dear friend Manuman's district. Miaki and Nouka's army burned the villages, killed all who came in their way, and carried away all the food and property they could. But at night they returned to keep watch over Nowar and me.

That very night Nowar declared that I must leave his village before morning or he and his people would be killed for protecting me. He advised me that the sea was good and to try for Mr. Mathieson's mission station. He objected to my taking any of my property along; he would soon follow with it himself. But how to sail? Miaki had stolen my boat, mast, sails, oars, and an excellent canoe. But the danger was too great, so Nowar urged, "You cannot remain longer in my house! My son will guide you to the large chestnut tree in my plantation in the bush. Climb up into it, and remain there till the moon rises."

Entirely at the mercy of such unstable friends, I obeyed. The hours I spent in that tree live before me as if they were yesterday. I heard the frequent discharging of muskets and the yells of the warriors. Yet I sat there among the branches, as safe as in the arms of Jesus! Never in all my sorrows did my Lord draw nearer to me than when the moonlight flickered among those chestnut leaves, and the night air played on my throbbing brow, as I told all my heart to Jesus.

About midnight Nowar sent his son to call me down from the tree and guide me to the shore where he said Nowar was waiting to send me off in a canoe. My life and the lives of my Aneityumese now hung upon a very slender thread. We were almost equally at risk from our friends and our enemies. Had I been a stranger to Jesus and to prayer, my reason would have given way. My only comfort and joy came from His promise, "I will never leave you or forsake you. I am with you always!" Pleading these promises, I followed my guide. We reached the beach at a beautiful white sandy bay on Nowar's ground.

After much arguing with a canoe's owner we finally got one. Then, ready to embark, Chief Faimungo came forward and said, "Missi, they are all deceiving you! The sea is so rough, you cannot go. And if you should get round the point, Miaki has men ready to shoot you there. By land all the paths are guarded by armed men."

My party of five now embarked in our frail canoe, since it was the only gleam of hope left to us. Abraham first, I next, Matthew after me, a boy at the steering paddle, and Abraham's wife sitting in the bottom. For a mile or more we got away nicely under the lee of the island, but when we turned to go south for Mr. Mathieson's station, we met the full force of wind and sea, every wave breaking over and almost swamping our canoe. We were forced to bail with all our might and turn back. After four more hours of a terrible struggle, we succeeded in again reaching smooth water toward daylight. With God's blessing we at last reached the shore, exactly where we had left it five hours earlier!

Now drenched and weary, with our hands sticking to the paddles, we left the canoe on the reef and waded ashore. The islanders looked sullen and disappointed at our return. The lad who had been with us instantly fled for his own land, and the islanders reported that he was murdered soon after. Utterly exhausted I lay down on the sand and instantly fell into a deep sleep. By and by I felt someone pulling from under my head the bag in which I carried my Bible and the Tannese translations—the only things I had saved. Grasping the bag I sprang to my feet, and the man ran away. My teachers had a hedging knife and a saltwater-soaked revolver and fowling piece, the sight of which God used to restrain the islanders. Calling the Aneityumese near, we kneeled on the sand and committed each other to the Lord God.

As I sat meditating, Faimungo, the friendly inland chief, came again to warn us of danger. All Nowar's men had fled, and Miaki was holding a meeting not half a mile away, preparing to attack us. Faimungo concluded, "Farewell, Missi, I am going home. I don't wish to see the murders this morning."

He was Nowar's son-in-law and had always been truthful and kind to me. His home was halfway across the island, on the road we wanted to take. Impulsively, I asked, "Faimungo, will you let us follow you? Will you show us the path? The hurricanes have destroyed the paths so that I wouldn't be able to find the way. When the mission ship arrives, I will give you three good axes, blankets, knives, fishhooks, and more."

He trembled and said, "Missi, you will be killed. Miaki will shoot you. I don't dare let you follow. I have only twenty men and your following would endanger us all."

I urged him to leave at once, and we would follow at a distance. I would not ask him to protect us, but if he betrayed us and helped the enemy kill us, I assured him that our God would punish him. He said, "Seven men are with me now. Since the other thirteen are with Miaki, I will not send for them. You may follow me as far as you can, but you will be killed on the way."

Though Nowar had a box of my rice and many goods from the plunder of my house, and though he had cooked two of my goats for himself and his people, he would not give any food to the starving Aneityumese or me, but hurried us off, saying, "I will eat all your rice and keep all that has been left with me in payment for my lame knee and for my people fighting for you!"

Collecting his share of my stolen property from Nowar, Faimungo called his seven men and off they ran. To avoid Miaki's men they ran through a large coconut grove skirting the shore. They called back, "Quickly! Follow and keep as near to us as you can."

We could place no confidence in any of them, but it appeared to be our only hope. So we started after them and got away unobserved by our enemies.

Four miles on our way, we met a large party of Miaki's men, all armed and watching as outposts. Some wanted to shoot us, but others hesitated. Every musket was raised and leveled at me. Faimungo poised his great spear and shouted, "No! You shall not kill Missi today! He is with me." Then he strode off after his own men, and the Aneityumese followed, leaving me face to face with a ring of leveled muskets. Their leader, Sirawia, once my friend, greeted me, "My love to you, Missi." Then he shouted after Faimungo, "Your conduct is bad in taking Missi away! Leave him with us to be killed!"

I turned on him saying, "Sirawia, I love you all. You know I sought only your good. I gave you medicine and food when you and your people were sick and dying with measles. I gave you the very clothing you wear. Am I not your friend? Haven't we often drunk tea and eaten together in my house? Can you stand there and see your friend shot? If you do, my God will punish you severely."

Then he whispered something to his company I could not hear. Their muskets stayed up, but their eyes had changed. I began gradually to move backward, still keeping my eyes fixed on them till the bush hid them from my view. Then I turned and ran after my party, and God kept the enemy from following.

Another party of the enemy encountered us and were eager for our lives. This time Faimungo withstood them firmly as his men encircled us. He said to me, "I am not afraid, Missi. I am feeling stronger near my own land!"

Hurrying onward we came to that village on their high ground called Aneai (heaven). The sun was oppressively hot, the path almost unshaded, and our whole party exhausted, especially Faimungo, who was carrying his load of stolen goods. He sat down on the village dancing ground for a smoke, saying, "Missi, I am near my own land now. We can rest with safety."

After a few minutes he jumped up in wild excitement. Over a mountain, behind the village and above it, there came shouting and the *tramp-tramp* of a multitude making rapidly toward us. Faimungo got up and planted his back against a tree. I stood beside him, and the Aneityumese woman and the two men stood near me while his men seemed prepared to flee. At full speed a large body of the tallest and most powerful men that I had seen on Tanna came rushing on and filled the dancing ground. They were all armed and flushed with their success in war. They had learned of our escape and had moved cross-country to intercept us. Faimungo was much afraid and said, "Missi, go quickly down that path, you and your Aneityumese. I will follow when I have had a smoke and a talk with these men."

I replied, "No, I will stand by your side till you go. If I am killed, it will be by your side. I will not leave you." He implored us to go on, but that would have been certain death.

The warriors began urging one another to kill us, but I looked among them as calmly as possible, saying, "My Jehovah God will punish you if you kill me or any of His servants."

A killing stone thrown by one of the savages grazed poor old Abraham's cheek. A club rose to follow the blow, but God baffled the aim. They encircled us in a deadly ring, and one kept urging another to strike the first blow or fire the first shot.

My heart rose up to the Lord Jesus, and I saw Him watching the scene. Peace came back to me like a wave from God. I realized I was immortal till my Master's work with me was done. The assurance came to me, as if a voice out of heaven had spoken, that not a musket would be fired, not a club would touch us, not a spear leave the hand, not an arrow leave the bow, or a killing stone the fingers, without the permission of Jesus Christ who has all power in heaven and on earth.

Yet I could never say that on such occasions I was without fear. I have felt my reason reeling, my sight coming and going, and my knees striking together when close to a violent death.

Faimungo and others now urged us to escape down the path. "Faimungo, why are we to leave you?" I asked. "My God heard your promise not to betray me. He knows now what is in your heart and in mine. I will not leave you. If I am to die, I will die by your side." His men had gone, and I had persuaded my Aneityumese to follow them.

"I will go on now," he replied. "Missi, keep close to me." With a bound, Faimungo started after his men. I kept as near him as I could, pleading with Jesus to protect me or take me home to glory. The host of armed men also ran along on each side with their weapons ready. Leaving everything to Jesus I ran on as if they were my escort or as if I did not see them. If anyone wonders how they were restrained, I wonder even more.

We came to a stream crossing our path. With a bound all my party cleared it, ran up the opposite bank, and disappeared into the bush. I tried the leap, but I struck the bank and slid back on my hands and knees toward the stream. At this moment I heard a crash above my head in an overhanging tree. A killing stone had been thrown but had lodged in a branch, and that branch had saved me. Praising God, I scrambled up the other side and followed the track of my party into the bush. The warriors gazed after me for a little in silence, but no one crossed the stream. One portion returned to the village, and the other pressed inland.

I caught up with my party resting in the bush—amazed to see me alive when the warriors had been so thirsty for my blood. Faimungo now ascended the mountain and kept away from the common path to avoid other bands. At every village, enemies of our worship were ready to shoot us. I kept close to our guide, knowing that the fear of shooting Faimungo would prevent anyone from shooting at me; he was the most influential chief in all that part of the island.

In our flight we passed springs and streams, but none of us dared to stoop down for a drink, though parched with sickening thirst. We would almost certainly have been killed in the act. Faimungo now sent some of his men home by a different path and guided us himself till we were near shore. Sitting down he said, "Missi, I have now fulfilled my promise. I am so tired and afraid. I dare not go farther. My love to you all. Now go on quickly! Three of my men will go with you to the next rocks. Go quickly! Farewell."

These men went on a little and then stopped, announcing, "Missi, we dare not go! Faimungo is at war with people of the next land. Just keep straight along this path." Then they turned and ran back to their own village.

As we hurried along the shore two young men

came running after us, raising their quivering spears. I took the useless revolver out of my little native basket and, raising it, cried, "Beware! Lay down your spears at once on the sand, and carry my basket to the next landing at the black rocks." They threw their spears on the sand, lifted the bag, and ran on before us to the rocks which marked their enemies' border. Laying the basket down, they pleaded, "Missi, let us return home!" And how they did run, fearing the pursuit of their foes.

With the blessing of Almighty God we drew near to Mr. Mathieson's station in safety. Here a man gave each of us a coconut, which we needed badly, having tasted nothing all that day, and very little for several days before. We were so weak that only the struggle for life enabled us to keep our feet. Yet the Aneityumese never complained and never halted.

Upon hearing our arrival, Mr. Mathieson came running to meet me. Mr. and Mrs. Mathieson had heard of our flight and thought we were dead! They were both very weak, having just laid their only child in the grave and now, on top of their great grief, had endured this great peril.

The next day we heard that three more of Manuman's people had been killed and a whole district burned. Four days later, on Sunday, thirty people came to worship at the mission house. Then, taking a great risk, we had worship services at three of the nearest and most friendly villages. We preached the Gospel to over one hundred people. It was sowing in tears, but who will say that it was in vain! Twenty years have passed, and now when I am writing this, there is a church of God singing the praises of Jesus in that very district of Tanna.

That week young Chief Kapuku came to Mr. Mathieson and handed over his own and his father's war gods and household idols. They consisted of a basket of small and peculiar stones, worn and shiny with use. He said, "While many are trying to kill you and drive the worship of Jehovah from this island, I give up my gods and will send away all heathen idols from my land."

Meanwhile a party of Miaki's men were canvasing Mr. Mathieson's district inciting people to kill us. Faimungo came to warn us that Miaki was exerting all his influence to destroy us. Chief Manuman sent Raki, his adopted son, to tell me of the fearful sufferings he and his people were now passing through—some were killed almost every day. Raki's wife, a chief's daughter, had returned to her father's care when Miaki attacked their tribe. Miaki's men had gone to that chief's house and forced Raki's father-in-law to give his daughter up as an enemy. They clubbed her to death and feasted on her.

The following Sunday thirty-two people attended the morning service. Mr. Mathieson and I, committing ourselves to Jesus, went inland and conducted worship at seven villages, preaching to about one hundred people. Nearly all appeared friendly. The people of one village had been persuaded to kill us on our return home, but God guided us to take another way and so we escaped.

The next day, a company of Miaki's men came to the mission house and forced Mrs. Mathieson to show them through the premises. Providentially, I had bolted myself that morning into a closet and was engrossed with writing. They went through every room in the house and, not seeing me, concluded I had gone inland. They discharged a musket into our teachers' house, then left quietly, greatly disappointed at not finding me. My heart soared in praise to God for another deliverance!

Deeply fatigued, I lay down early that night and fell into a deep sleep. About ten o'clock, the warriors surrounded the mission house. My faithful dog, Clutha, sprang quietly upon me. Pulling at my clothes, she woke me to warn me of the danger. Silently I woke the Mathiesons, and we committed ourselves in prayer to God. Suddenly a glare of light fell into the room! Men passed with flaming torches—they set fire to the church and then to a reed fence connecting the church and the house. In a few minutes the house too would be in flames, and armed men were waiting to kill us if we attempted escape! Taking my harmless revolver in the left hand and a little American tomahawk in the right, I pleaded with Mr. Mathieson to let me out and instantly lock the door on himself and his wife. "Stop here and let us die together!" he said, grabbing on to me. "You will never return!"

"Leave that to God," I said. "In a few minutes our house will be in flames, and then nothing can save us."

I ran to the burning reed fence, cut it from top to bottom, tore it up, and threw it back into the flames so that the fire could not follow it to our house. I saw shadows on the ground; I looked up and seven or eight warriors had surrounded me with their clubs raised in the air. I heard a shout, "Kill him! Kill him!" One seized for me, but I leaped from his clutches and drew the revolver from my pocket. I leveled it at them, my heart going up in prayer to God, and challenged them, "Dare to strike me, and my Jehovah God will punish you—for burning His church, for hatred to His worship and His people, and for all your bad conduct. We love all of you. For doing only good you want to kill us. But our God is here to protect us and He will do just that."

They yelled in rage and urged each other to strike the first blow, but the Invisible One restrained them. At this dreadful moment a rushing and roaring sound came from the south. Every head instinctively turned, knowing it was one of their awful storms. As it came suddenly upon us, the mighty roaring of the wind and unceasing torrents awed my attackers into silence. Some began to withdraw from the scene. All lowered their weapons of war, and, terror-stricken, several exclaimed, "This is Jehovah's rain! Their Jehovah God is fighting for them and helping them. Run! Run!" A panic seized them as they threw away their torches and disappeared into the bush. I was left alone praising God for His marvelous works.

The wind blew the flames away from our house. If it had come in the other direction, no power on earth could have saved us all from being consumed! The rain that followed the wind made it almost impossible now to set fire to our house.

All through the remainder of that night I lay wide awake keeping watch, my noble little dog lying near me with ears alert. Early in the morning friends came weeping. Our enemies were loudly celebrating. They had firmly resolved to kill us at

once, to plunder our house and then burn it. The
noise of their shouting could be plainly heard as
they neared the mission premises. Our friendly,
weeping islanders looked terrified. Just then we
heard, or dreamed that we heard, a cry higher still,
"Sail-O!"

We were by this time beginning to distrust almost our very senses, but again and again that cry
came rolling up from the shore, "Sail-O!" And it was
repeated from crowd to crowd all along the beach,
"Sail-O! Sail-O!" The shouts of our approaching
murderers gradually ceased, and the whole group
melted away from our view. I feared some cruel de-
ception and peered out very cautiously. But there it
was—a ship had sailed into the bay. I set fire to the
reeds on the side of our hill to attract its attention.
I put a black shawl on one end of the mission house
as a flag and a white sheet on the other.

Twenty armed Aneityumese came on shore in
two boats. The ship had gotten news about us from
our own harbor on the other side of the island and
sailed right past to Aneityum, the crew dressed in
my looted shirts. The missionaries there had persuaded the boat's owner to send this party to rescue
us, if we were still alive to be rescued.

We had the boats loaded and ready to start by
two in the afternoon, when Mr. Mathieson locked
himself up and refused to go. Apparently suffering
from a nervous collapse, he had resolved to stay behind and die on Tanna. We told him the inconsis-
tency of praying to God to protect us and then refusing His rescue. Surely it was better to live and
work for Jesus than to die as a self-made martyr.
His wife wept aloud and pleaded with him too, but

all in vain. Finally I said, "It is getting dark. Your wife must go with the ship, but I will not leave you alone. I will send a note explaining why I am forced to stay. It is certain that we will be murdered when the vessel leaves, and God will charge you with both our deaths." At this he relented and unlocked the door.

We hurried to the boats and left immediately. Having lost several hours, the ship had drifted out, away from sight in the darkness. After some time of aimless floating, both boats set off for Port Resolution to await the ship's arrival, steering by the flame of the volcano, a never-failing lighthouse visible for fifty miles.

As light appeared we anchored as far out as possible, beyond the reach of Miaki's muskets. We sat under a tropical sun all morning without water or food, and still there was no ship. The leader put all the passengers and the weakest seamen into one boat and left us to swing at anchor. With a strong crew in the other, he started off in search of the ship.

In the afternoon Nowar and Miaki came out in a canoe to visit us. They urged me to go and see the mission house, but we had seen a body of men near it and so refused to go. Miaki declared that everything remained as I had left it, but we knew he was lying. Old Abraham had slipped on to shore in a canoe and found the windows smashed and everything gone but a few of my books, which were scattered and torn. Armed men there had wanted to kill him, but others said, "Not till we can kill Missi too!"

About five o'clock in the evening the ship appeared. Before dark we were all safely on board and sailing for Aneityum. Though both Mr. and Mrs. Mathieson had become very weak, they stood the voyage wonderfully. Next day we were all safely landed. We had offered the captain payment for our trip, but he declined any fare. We divided the money among the mate and crew, for they had all shown great kindness to us on the voyage. After arriving on Aneityum, Mrs. Mathieson gradually sank under tuberculosis and fell asleep in Jesus in mid-March. Mr. Mathieson, more and more depressed after his wife's death, died in mid-June, still trusting Jesus.

My own intention was to remain on Aneityum, go on with my work of translating the Gospels, and watch for the earliest opportunity to return to Tanna. I was very weak and thin, however, my health undoubtedly shaken by the continuous stress and danger of the last several months on Tanna. The other missionaries united in urging me to promote our mission in Australia and to seek to acquire a ship there for the mission's use. Reluctantly, I left my dear islanders for a season.

7

Australia to Aniwa

I did not know one person in Sydney, Australia. Due to a denominational dispute I had to strike out on my own as no minister would allow me to speak to his congregation or Sunday school. On impulse, I followed a group of children into a Sunday school. At the close I went up and asked for ten minutes to speak to them. After a little hesitation they gave me fifteen minutes. Becoming deeply interested, the minister then invited me to preach to his congregation that evening. Shortly I had access to almost every church and Sunday school, both Presbyterian and independent.

A few of the most friendly ministers formed themselves into a committee for the mission ship. Our dear Lord Jesus opened up my way so that now I had more church invitations than I could accept, and the monetary response was beyond expectation.

I made children shareholders in the new mission ship—receiving printed forms at sixpence each. Thousands of these shares were taken. The ship was to be the children's very own. They launched a great shipping company for Jesus.

109

I addressed three or four meetings every Sunday, and one or more every weekday, traveling over the length and breadth of Victoria, Tasmania, and South Australia. The quick progress led us to aim at a ship three times the size of our original proposition. I vowed in private that if God sent in a certain additional sum by a given date, that would be my Gideon's fleece. I would then go home to Scotland and recruit more missionaries for the islands.

Returning to Melbourne, I reported all to the committee, including the fleece. One member stood to his feet and affirmed, "Sir, this whole work is God's and not ours. Go home, and He will give you more missionaries for the islands." Dr. Inglis, just returned from Britain where he had printed the Aneityumese New Testament, also urged me to go.

Yet my path was far from clear. To lose time in going home to do work that others ought to do could hardly be my duty. Finding no light, I took a step that I had only done once. Some will mock, but others may see faith in it. After many prayers and tears I went alone before the Lord and on my knees cast lots with a solemn appeal to God. The answer came: Go home! I sincerely believe that on both these occasions the Lord condescended to decide for me the path of duty. I believe it more certainly now in view of the outcome of thirty years of service to Christ that flowed out of those steps. In this and in many other matters, I am no law to others. Nor can I refrain from adding that, for the very reasons indicated above, I regard lotteries and raffles as a mockery of God and little if at all short of blasphemy.

So I sailed off for Britain on the sixteenth of

May, 1863. We cast anchor safely at London on the twenty-sixth of August, 1863, at 5:30 P.M. I had never been to London, and I would have enjoyed its palaces and memorials. But the King's business entrusted to me required haste, and I felt the need to press on. At nine o'clock that evening I left for Scotland by train. Next morning, about nine, I reported to the head of the foreign mission committee and arranged a meeting of the committee.

By the next train I was on my way to Dumfries, and then to my dear old home at Torthorwald. There I had a heavenly welcome from my saintly parents, accompanied by many fast-falling tears. Only five brief years had elapsed since I had left their sanctuary with my young bride. Now that grave on Tanna held wife and son locked in each other's embrace till Resurrection Day. Just as warm, but terribly agonizing, was my reception by my bride's parents a few days later. Their hearts had broken, and they never fully recovered.

My church's foreign mission committee welcomed me warmly to their meeting in Edinburgh. They agreed at once to my visiting and addressing every Sunday school in the church. They invited me to speak to their seminary students. Generously and enthusiastically they gave all in their power to help me.

At the close of my tour one in every six of my church's ministers was a missionary. Nor did the dear church cripple herself. Her zeal for missions accompanied, if not caused, new prosperity at home. Debts that had burdened many churches were swept away. New congregations were started.

Sunday school children became shareholders in

the mission ship as a *Dayspring* collection box
found its way into almost every family. Four new
missionaries volunteered for the islands from Scotland, and three from Nova Scotia. Together, we not
only reclaimed for Jesus the posts that had been
abandoned, but we started on new islands. I did not
wait to take them with me because they had im-
portant things to learn first in theology and medicine.

Yet I did not return alone. The dear Lord
brought me a specially prepared partner to share
my lot on the islands. Her heart stirred with a
yearning to teach those sitting in darkness. Her
brother had died young as a missionary, and her
sister and brother-in-law were also missionaries.
Before I left Scotland in 1864, I was married to
Margaret Whitecross, and God spares us to each
other still. We have dedicated our children to His
service, with the hope that He may use every one of
them in spreading the Gospel throughout the lost
world.

My last scene in Scotland was kneeling at the
family altar in the old sanctuary cottage. My father,
with his snow-white hair streaming over his shoulders, commended us once again to God's care. It was
the last time on earth his prayers would fall on my
ears. I knew beyond doubt that when we rose from
our knees and said farewell, our eyes would never
meet again till they were flooded with the light of
Resurrection Day. Still, he and my darling mother
gave us away with a free heart, not without pain,
to the service of our common Lord and to the salvation of the lost. My beloved mother fell asleep in
1865, and my priest-like father passed on in 1868,

in his seventy-seventh year.

My wife and I met the *Dayspring* in Australia in January 1865 and rode her down to the islands. I reported all my experiences at the missionaries' annual meeting. They sent me to Australia again to raise funds for the *Dayspring*'s support and maintenance. The Lord seemed to leave me no alternative. With great reluctance, I turned my back to the islands again.

Arriving at Sydney, I was at once plunged into a whirlpool of horrors. The H.M.S. *Curacao* had just punished an island for murder and robbery of traders. As usual, missionaries had been drafted as interpreters, and of course used their influence on the side of mercy. But Australia and the Western world were thrown into a ferment just a few days before our arrival by inflammatory articles and illustrations in a leading newspaper: The *Curacao* was pictured lying off the shore with the *Dayspring* in tow. The Tannese warriors were being blown to pieces by shot and shell and lay in bloody heaps on the shore. The missionaries were shown safe in the man-of-war, directing the onslaught and gloating over the carnage. The shocking news had been telegraphed to Britain and America.

That evening my reply, denying that such battles ever took place and detailing the actual facts of which I had been an eyewitness, was in the hands of the editor. I also hinted that legal prosecution would be forthcoming unless a total withdrawal and apology were published at once. The newspaper printed my rejoinder and made satisfactory amends. This painful affair cost me dear personal friends, but my esteem for them did not change.

The plan for meeting the yearly upkeep of the *Dayspring* was to provide missionary coin boxes for Sunday school children. In organizing and maturing this scheme, I spoke to almost every Presbyterian congregation and Sunday school in Australia and Tasmania. The Lord sent what was required to keep the *Dayspring* carrying the Gospel and His servants among the islands—unstained with the polluting and bloody associations of the trading ships!

On this tour, in Victoria alone, I spent 250 days and addressed 265 meetings in 180 different churches. The proportion was on the same scale in the other areas visited. And all these arrangements I had to make for myself, by painful and laborious correspondence night and day. The Presbyterian Church of Victoria adopted me as a missionary in 1866—its first missionary to the Islands.

One of the bitterest trials of my life was not being allowed to return and settle on dear Tanna. I was sent to Aniwa (a-NEE-wa) instead, Tanna's nearest neighbor, hoping that God would soon open the way back to bloodstained Tanna. My heart bleeds for the lost, and I long to see a teacher for every tribe and a missionary for every one of the Islands. The hope still burns that I may witness it; then I could gladly rest.

On the way to Aniwa, we planted missionaries here and there, to the wonder of the islanders. "How is this?" they cried. "We killed or drove them all away! We plundered their houses and robbed them. If we had been treated like that, nothing could make us return. But you come back in a beautiful new ship and with more and more missionaries. If your God makes you do that, we may yet worship Him too." In this way island after island each received a missionary, and their chiefs bound themselves to protect and care for them.

The *Dayspring* called at Tanna too. Many memories revived again—wounds that still bleed afresh as I write, twenty-five years later. Nowar, the old chief, unstable but friendly, was determined to keep us there by force or fraud. The captain told him the council of missionaries had forbidden him to land our boxes on Tanna.

"Don't land them," said the wily chief. "Just throw them over. My men and I will catch everything before it touches the water and carry it all safely ashore." At the captain's refusal, Nowar tried again, "Then just point out his boxes for us. You will have no further trouble. We will manage everything for Missi."

They were in distress when he refused, and poor old Nowar tried another tack. Suspecting that my dear wife was afraid of the Tannese, he got us on shore to see his extensive plantations. Turning eagerly to her, he began talking and counted on me to interpret, "Plenty of food! While I have a yam or a banana, you will not lack."

She answered, "I do not fear running out of food."

Pointing to his warriors he cried, "We are many! We are strong! We can always protect you."

"I am not afraid," she calmly replied.

He then led us to the tree where I sat the night of my flight, when all hope of earthly deliverance had perished. He spoke to her with sincere emotion,

"The God who protected Missi there will always protect you."

She assured him that she had no fear of that kind, but that we must for now go to Aniwa. We would return to Tanna if the Lord opened our way. Nowar, Arkurat, and the rest seemed genuinely grieved, and it touched my soul to the quick.

The beautiful conclusion to this episode remained hidden from us for many years: One of the great sacred chiefs from Aniwa was visiting Tanna at this time. He and his people had been promised passage home on the *Dayspring* with their canoes in tow. When old Nowar saw that he could not keep us with himself, he went to this Aniwan chief. He took the white shells of chieftainship from his own arm and bound them to the Aniwan, saying, "By these you promise to protect my missionary and his wife and child on Aniwa. Let no evil come to them, or by this pledge, I and my people will avenge it."

In a future crisis this probably saved our lives. After all, a bit of Christ's Spirit had found its way into that old cannibal's soul! And the same Spirit in me yearned more strongly still, making it painful to leave Tanna and him in that dim, groping twilight of the soul.

Miaki continued in his intense hatred for the more righteous Nowar, Manuman, Sirawia, and Faimungo. Yet long after death had swept away Miaki and their other enemies, these four friendly chiefs survived. Nowar, Manuman, and Sirawia lived to be very old men, and to the last they professed Christ, though their knowledge was very limited and their inconsistencies grave and frequent. Happily, we are not the judges, deciding how many and what things may be forgiven. We do not pronounce whether there is or is not that spark of love, that grain of faith which the Lord, in His mercy, will freely accept and multiply.

Aniwa became my mission home in November 1866 and still is, except on my too-frequent pilgrimages among churches in the West. It has been the heart and center of my personal labors among the lost. God never guided me back to Tanna, but others, my dear friends, have seen His kingdom planted and beginning to grow among that slowly relenting race. I claimed Aniwa for Jesus, and by God's grace Aniwa now worships at the Savior's feet.

The island of Aniwa is one of the smaller isles of Vanuatu. It measures about nine miles by three and a half and is surrounded all around by a belt of coral reef. The sea breaks heavily on the reef with a thundering roar, and when the white surf rolls in it is furious and far-reaching. But there are days of calm, when the sea is glass, and the spray on the reef is a delicate fringe of silver.

No stone or other rock appears anywhere on the island—only the coral, in its beautiful and mysterious variety. The highest land is less than three hundred feet above the sea. Though the soil is generally light, there are deep patches toward the island's southern end, near the crater of an extinct volcano. There excellent plantations grow and could support ten times the present population.

Aniwa suffers badly from inadequate rainfall. The heavy rains of hurricane and tempest disappear as if by magic through the light soil and porous rock. But the moist atmosphere and the heavy dews keep the island green, and large fruit trees draw nourishment from below. The islanders themselves suffer from a species of elephantiasis.

I knew little of Aniwa before we arrived. I had glimpsed it once before, when passing on a ship. And I had seen Aniwans in their canoes at Tanna in search of food. They had then pleaded with us to live among them, arguing against two missionary couples on Tanna and none on Aniwa. Virtually everything had to be learned afresh on Aniwa, just as on Tanna.

When we landed, the islanders received us kindly. They and the Aneityumese teachers led us to a temporary home they had prepared. Walls and roof consisted of sugarcane leaf and reeds intertwined on a strong wooden frame. There were neither doors nor windows in the house, but only holes for them in the walls. The floor, however, looked beautiful, covered thick with white coral broken small. There was but one room that had to serve for church, school, and public hall. We screened off a little portion where we planted our bed and stored our valuables until we could build our own house. All the islanders around came to watch us eat our meals! Our chairs were boxes, and the lid of another box was our table. Our cooking was all done in the open air under a large tree, and we got along in amazing comfort.

They did not steal like the Tannese, but their requests to borrow things were sometimes underlined with the swinging of a tomahawk. We tried to get along quietly and kindly, hoping that when we knew their language, they would be eager to hear about and know Jesus. Then life and property would be safe. The rumor of the *Curacao*'s visit and her punishment of murder and robbery did more to protect us during those early days than all other things combined.

Sorrowful experience on Tanna had taught us to seek the site for our Aniwan house on the highest ground, away from the malarial swamps near the shore. The most charming mound held a view of both Tanna and Erromanga, but the Aniwans would not let us build there. They forced us to build on other high ground nearer the shore. When we cleared away the mounds on top of this site, we found the bones and refuse of their cannibal feasts. After leveling the site and gently sloping its sides for good drainage, I had gathered two large baskets of human bones. I asked a chief in Tannese, "How did these bones get here?"

He replied with a shrug, "We are not Tanna men! We don't eat the bones!"

My wife and I debated whether to build only a temporary home, hoping to return to dear old Tanna as soon as possible, or, though the work would be much harder, a solid house, for the comfort of our successors if not for ourselves. Since this was God's work, we decided to make it the very best we could. We initially planned two central rooms, sixteen feet by sixteen, with a five-foot lobby between, for future expansion. About a quarter mile from the sea and thirty-five feet above it, I laid the foundation for the house. Coral blocks raised the walls about three feet high all around. Air passages carried sweeping currents underneath each room to lessen the risk of fever and ague. We dug a wide trench all around and filled it up as a drain with broken coral. At the back and front, the veranda stretched five feet wide. Pantry, bathroom, and tool-house were partitioned off under the veranda behind. The windows sent to me had hinges. I added two feet vertically to each, with wood from shipping boxes, and made them French doors, opening from each room to the veranda. At last we had, by God's blessing, a healthy spot to live in if not exactly a thing of beauty.

Eventually the mission house had six rooms, three on each side of the lobby, which measured ninety feet in length, and all was surrounded by a veranda, one hundred feet by five, which kept everything shaded and cool. Under two rooms, we dug a cellar eight feet deep with shelving all around for storage. In more than one hurricane that cellar saved our lives. We would all squeeze into it when trees and houses were being tossed like feathers on the wings of the wind.

As on Tanna all sicknesses and deaths were thought to be caused by sorcery, there called *nahak*, on Aniwa called *tafigeitu*. Some sacred men burned the remains of food such as the skin of a banana, or a hair from the head, or even something the person had touched to bring disease to that person. When someone became sick all the people in his village met day after day to make long speeches and find out which enemy was causing it. Having focused on someone, they first sent presents of mats, baskets, and food to the appropriate disease-makers. If the person recovered the sacred men took credit for it. If the person died, his friends sought revenge on the supposed murderers. Such revenge took a wide sweep, satisfying itself with the suspected enemy, or anyone in his family, village, or even from his tribe. And so endless bloodshed and intertribal wars kept the people in turmoil from one end of the island to the other.

Still we set our bell to ringing every day after dinner, announcing our readiness to give advice or medicine to any who were sick. We spoke to them, as soon as we had learned their language, a few words about Jesus. The weak gratefully received a cup of tea and a piece of bread. The demand was great, especially when epidemics struck. Others fled from us, thinking we were the cause of their sickness, rushing off at our approach and hiding in the bush.

Learning the language on Aniwa was slightly easier than on Tanna since a few could understand my Tannese. It was, however, largely the same process. One day a man carefully examined something and then said to his neighbor, *"Taha tinei?"*

I inferred he was asking, "What is this?"

Pointing to another object I repeated the words. They smiled at each other and gave me its name. On another occasion, a man said to his companion while looking at me, *"Taha neigo?"*

Concluding that he was asking my name, I pointed toward him and repeated the words, and they at once gave me their names. It is surprising how much you can learn with these two short questions constantly on your lips and with people everywhere you go ready to answer: What is this? and, What is your name?

We wrote down every word at once, phonetically

and in alphabetical order, with a note on the circumstances in which it was used. By frequent comparison of these notes, and by careful daily and hourly imitation of all their sounds, we learned to understand each other before we had gone far in building the house.

While building our house, I ran out of nails and needed some tools too. I penciled a few words on a piece of planed wood and requested our old chief to carry it to my wife. "She will send what I want," I said.

In blank wonder, he stared at me and asked, "But what do you want?"

"The wood will tell her," I replied.

"Who ever heard of wood talking?" he snapped. He looked rather angry, thinking I was fooling him.

I pleaded with the chief, and finally he went. He was amazed to see my wife look at the wood and then fetch the needed supplies. He brought back the piece of wood and eagerly asked for an explanation. I read the words to him and told him that in the same way God speaks to us through His Book. As soon as he learned to read, he would hear God speaking to him from the Bible, as Mrs. Paton heard me from the bit of wood.

A great desire awakened in the chief to see the Word of God printed in his own language. He helped me to learn words and master his language. And when my work of translating portions of the Bible began, his delight was unbounded!

Our mission house was repeatedly threatened with fire, and ourselves with muskets, before the house was done. The threats to set fire to our house stirred up Chief Namakei to befriend us. He and his people guarded us by night and by day. Still, a savage Erromangan lurked about for ten days, watching for us with tomahawk and musket, and we knew that our peril was extreme. Looking to God for protection I went on with my daily work showing no fear—and with a small American tomahawk beside me. My main focus was to take every precaution against surprise because these murderers would try nothing when observed. I finally sent for the old chief who was the Erromangan's host and warned him that God would hold him guilty if our blood was shed. "Missi," he replied warmly, "I didn't know! I didn't know! By the first favorable wind he will go, and you won't see him again." The chief kept his word, and we were rescued again.

The mission station, with its surrounding grounds, came along wonderfully. The pathway up to it was adorned on each side with beautiful shrubs and island plants, and behind these a row of orange trees. A coconut grove skirted the shore for nearly three miles and shaded the main public road. Near our premises were many leafy chestnuts and wide-spreading breadfruit trees. As years went by we lived practically in the middle of a lovely village with all conveniences: church, school, orphanage, smithy and carpenter's shop, printing office, banana and yam house, cookhouse. The little road leading to each door was laid with white coral, broken small. The fence around all shone fresh and clean with new paint.

At first we had not known why they forced this building site on us. After Chief Namakei became a Christian, he revealed the reason in a message to the Aniwans, "When Missi came we saw his boxes.

We knew he had blankets and calico, axes and knives, fishhooks and all such things. We said, 'Don't drive him off or we will lose all these things. We will let him land. But we will force him to live on the sacred plot. Our gods will kill him, and we will divide all that he has among ourselves.' Missi built his house on our most sacred spot, touching all those deadly bones that only our sacred men can touch. He and his people lived there, and the gods did not strike. He planted bananas there, and we said, 'Now when they eat of these they will all drop down dead, as our fathers assured us about anyone who eats fruit from that ground, anyone except our own sacred men.' These bananas ripened. The missionaries ate them. We kept watching for days and days, but no one died! Therefore, what we have said, and what our fathers said, is not true. Our gods cannot kill them. Their Jehovah God is stronger than the god of Aniwa!"

The old chief then led them in prayer—a strange, dark, groping prayer, with streaks of dark religion coloring every thought and sentence, but still a heartbreaking prayer. It was the cry of a soul once cannibal, but now being thrilled through and through with the first conscious pulsations of Christ's Spirit throbbing into the words, "Father, Father, our Father. . . ." Nothing will ever persuade me that the Divine Heart in heaven was not rejoicing too.

8

Beyond Revenge

Shortly before our arrival on Aniwa, an Aneityumese teacher had been murdered. The story shows how the Aniwans worship revenge. Many years ago, a party of Aniwans had gone to Aneityum on a friendly visit. The Aneityumese murdered and ate every man except one who escaped into the bush. Living on coconuts, he awaited a favorable wind and, launching his canoe by night, he arrived home safely. The Aniwans were enraged at his story and committed themselves to revenge. Since the forty-five miles of sea between them prevented a counterattack, they made a deep cut in the earth and vowed to renew that cut from year to year till the day of revenge came around. In this way they had kept the memory of the event alive for nearly eighty years.

When the Aneityumese came to know Jesus Christ, they yearned to spread that life-changing good news to the islands all around. They chose two of their leading men to go as teachers to Aniwa, Navalak, and Nemeyan, while others went to Fotuna, Tanna, and Erromanga. Namakei, the head chief of Aniwa, promised to protect and be kind to Navalak and Nemeyan. As time went on, it was discovered that the teachers belonged to the tribe on Aneityum—one of them to the very district where long ago the Aniwans had been murdered. The teachers had known their danger from the beginning but were eager to pass on the Gospel. The Aniwans resolved to kill the Aneityumese, but they had promised to protect them. So they hired two Tannese men and an Aniwan chief whose parents were Tannese to ambush and shoot the teachers as they returned from their circuit of villages on a Sunday afternoon. The assassins' muskets failed to fire, so they rushed upon the teachers with clubs and left them for dead.

Nemeyan was dead, another martyr. Poor Navalak was still breathing, and Chief Namakei carried him to his village and nursed him back to health. He pleaded with his people that the inherited claims of revenge had been satisfied and that Navalak should be sent home; Christ's Spirit was beginning to work in that darkened soul! Navalak is now a high chief on Aneityum. Often since, he has visited Aniwa and praised the Lord among the very people who once thirsted for his blood and left him for dead!

The first Aniwan to love Jesus was old Chief Namakei. We lived on his land, and his people were friendly to us. (His only brother, however, did try to shoot me on two different occasions.) At first Namakei likely came to our house only for our tea, for he left quickly afterward. But his interest grew until he showed great delight in helping us in every possible way. Along with him came Chief Naswai and his wife Katua. These three grew into the knowledge of Jesus together, and we came to love them deeply.

A widower, Namakei brought his little daughter Litsi Sore (Litsi the Great) to us. She was his only child and the queen of her race. He said, "I want to leave my Litsi with you. I want you to train her for Jesus." She was intelligent and soon became quite a help to my wife. Then the chief's brother, the sacred man that had twice tried to shoot me, also brought his daughter, Litsi Sisi (Litsi the Little), to be trained like her cousin. His wife too was dead. The children reported all they saw and learned to their fathers. They in turn became more interested in our work, and the Gospel spread far and wide. Soon we had many orphans committed to us. Many of them grew up as teachers and evangelists.

In our frequent dangers in those early times on Aniwa, our orphans often warned us privately and saved our lives from cruel plots. When, in baffled rage, our enemies demanded who had revealed things to us, I always said, "It was a little bird from the bush." Learning we would not betray them, the dear children grew to have perfect confidence in us. They considered themselves the guardians of our lives.

Excitement increased for everyone when a few men openly gave up their idols. But morning after morning I noticed green coconut leaves piled at the end of our house and wondered if they were connected to some sorcery. One night I learned the truth when an old chief knocked on the door and called, "Get up, Missi, and help! They are trying to burn your home. All night we have kept them off, but they are many and we are few. Get up quickly,

and light a lamp at every window. Let's pray to Jehovah and talk loudly as if we are many. God will
make us strong."

They had all my buckets and pails full of water.
The surrounding bush was swarming with warriors, torches in hand. The coconut leaves I had seen
were their protection from the heavy dew. After
that I took my turn with them in watching, each
guard changing after so many hours. Then they
said among themselves, "If our Missi is shot or
killed in the dark, what will we have to watch for
then? We must make Missi stay indoors at night!"
I gave up taking shifts but still went among them
watch by watch to encourage them.

———

My printing press on Tanna had been destroyed
and melted down for ammunition. I had gotten the
remains of one from Erromanga; the Gordons had
used it before they were murdered. Many letters
were missing, however, so that I could only print
four pages at a time. Other pieces of the press were
gone too, but I made substitutes from iron and wood
scraps. I printed an Aniwan hymnbook, a portion of
Genesis in Aniwan, a small book in Erromangan for
the new missionary, and other assorted things.

Chief Namakei eagerly helped me in translating
and preparing the first book. It had short passages
from the Scriptures to introduce them to God's
truth and love. Namakei came morning after morning, saying, "Missi, is it done? Can it speak?"

At last I could answer, "Yes!"

The old chief eagerly asked, "Does it speak my
words?"

"It does."

"Make it speak to me, Missi! Let me hear it speak." I read him a little bit, and he shouted in ecstasy, "It does speak! It speaks my own language too! Oh, give it to me!" He grabbed it, turned it all around every way, pressed it to his bosom, and then closing it with a look of great disappointment, handed it back to me, saying, "Missi, I cannot make it speak! It will never speak to me."

"I will teach you to read, Namakei. Then it will speak to you as it does to me."

"O Missi, dear Missi, show me how to make it speak!" he begged. He seemed to be straining his eyes, and I wondered if he could see the letters. So, I got out a pair of spectacles for him, but he was afraid of putting them on at first. When he got them on, he shouted excitedly, "I see it all now! This is what you told us about Jesus. He opened the eyes of a blind man. The word of Jesus has just come to Aniwa. He has sent me these glass eyes. I have gotten back again the sight I had when I was a boy. O Missi, make the book speak to me now!"

I walked out with him to the public village ground. There I drew A, B, and C in large characters in the dust and showed him the same letters in the book and left him to compare them and see how many were on the first page.

Before long he came running back to me and said, "I have lifted up A, B, and C. They are here in my head, and I will hold on to them. Give me three more." We repeated this time after time. He mastered the alphabet and soon began to spell out the smaller words. He had me read the book so often that he memorized it before he could read it. When people walked by him, he would get out the little book and say, "Come, and I will let you hear how the book speaks our own Aniwan words. You say it is hard to learn to read and make a book speak. Be strong and try! If an old man like me has done it, it ought to be much easier for you." He became our right-hand helper in the conversion of Aniwa.

Next, after God's own Word, the power of music was the strongest force for opening up our way. Namakei's wife positively shuddered at coming near the mission house. One day she heard Mrs. Paton playing on the little organ and singing a hymn in Aniwan. She came closer and closer, drinking in the music. After a while she ran off, and we thought she was afraid. But she was calling the women and girls from her village "to hear the box sing." She returned with them all at her heels, and they listened with dancing eyes. The sound of a hymn on the "box" always brought them flocking to class or a meeting.

Destitute of the power of singing, all my work would have been sadly hindered without my wife. They would never have known this joyous side of worship. She led our songs of praise both in the family and in the church. It was the first avenue by which Christianity winged its way into the hearts of the islanders.

One morning at daylight an islander came running to us in great excitement. Wielding his club furiously, he shouted, "Missi, I have killed the Tebil [devil]. I have killed Teapolo. He came to catch me last night. I woke up all the people, and we fought him 'round the house with our clubs. At daybreak he came out, and I killed him dead. We will have no more bad conduct or trouble now—Teapolo is dead!"

"What nonsense!" I retorted. "The devil is a spirit and cannot be seen."

In wild excitement he persisted that he had killed him. At my wife's advice I went with the man, and he led me to a great sacred rock of coral near our old hut. On it lay the dead body of a huge and beautiful serpent. "See," the man cried, "there he is! Yes, I have killed him."

I protested, "That is not the devil. It is only the body of a serpent."

"It is all the same! He is Teapolo. He makes us bad and causes all our troubles."

Following up on this hint, I began to investigate and learned that they associated man's troubles and sufferings with the serpent. They worshiped the serpent as a spirit of evil under the name of Matshiktshiki. They lived in terror of his influence, and all their worship was aimed at satisfying his rage against them. He figures strongly in their story of Creation.

They say that Matshiktshiki fished up these lands out of the sea. They point as proof to the deep print of his foot on the coral rocks opposite each island. There he stood as he strained and lifted the islands above the water. He then threw his great fishing line around Fotuna, thirty-six miles away, to draw it close to Aniwa and make them one land. As he pulled the line broke and he fell into the sea— so these islands remain separated to this day.

Matshiktshiki placed men and women on Aniwa. On the southern end of the island there was a beautiful spring and a freshwater river with rich lands all around for plantations. When the people didn't obey Matshiktshiki, he got so angry he split off the richer part of Aniwa with the spring and river and sailed across to Aneityum, leaving them there. That river is still called "the water of Aniwa" by the people of both islands. It is the ambition of all Aniwans to visit Aneityum and drink of that spring and river, as they sigh to each other, "O for the waters of Aniwa!"

Their picture of the Flood is equally grotesque. Long ago, when the volcano on Tanna was part of Aniwa, the rain fell and fell day after day, and the sea rose till it threatened to cover everything. All were drowned except the few who climbed up on this volcano mountain; the sea had already put out the other volcano at the southern end of Aniwa. Matshiktshiki lived in the larger volcano, and he became afraid that his big fire would go out too. So he split off that volcano from Aniwa with all the land on the southeastern side and sailed it across to Tanna on the tide of the flood. By his mighty strength he heaved the volcano to the top of the highest mountain in Tanna, where it remains to this day. When the sea went down he was not able to bring his big fire back to Aniwa. And so Aniwa is a very small island, with no volcano and no river.

Where there are no snakes the islanders apply the superstitions about the serpent to a large, black, poisonous lizard called *kekvau*. They call it Teapolo, and women and children scream wildly at the sight of one. Many of the islanders have the form of a lizard, a snake, a bird, or a man's face cut deep into the flesh of their arms. When the cuts begin to heal, they tear open the figures and press back the skin and force out the flesh—till the forms stand out above the skin and stay there as a visible horror for the rest of their lives. When they become Christians and put on clothing, they are anxious to cover these reminders of dark religion.

The most hideous blot on their societies is the practice of infanticide. Only three cases came to our knowledge on Aniwa. We publicly denounced them and awoke both natural feeling and the selfish interest of the community for the protection of the children. These three were the last that died there by parents' hands. A young husband, who had been jealous of his wife, buried their male child as soon as he was born. An old Tanna woman with no children living at last bore a fine healthy boy, and then threw him into the sea before anyone could interfere to save him. An angry husband snatched his baby from his wife's arms, hid himself in the bush till nighttime, and returned without the child. He gave no explanation except that the child was dead and buried. Praise God, these three murderers of their own children were all touched by the story of Jesus. They joined the church and adopted orphan children, to whom they showed the most tender affection and care.

Wife murder was also considered legitimate. In one of our inland villages lived a young couple, very happy except that they had no children. The husband, not a Christian, told his young wife that he had decided to bring home another wife, a widow with two children. His young wife naturally disapproved. Without warning, while she sat weaving a basket, he discharged a ball into her with his musket. It crashed through her arm and lodged in her side. I did all in my power to save her life, but on the tenth day tetanus came on. She soon passed away. The man had seemed devoted to her, but he insisted that she had no right to oppose his wishes! He was not punished or disrespected by the people of the village at all. A few weeks later he took home the widow as his wife. His second wife began to attend church and school regularly with her children. After a while the husband came along and had changed dramatically. The two have a large family and are earnestly trying to train all their children for the Lord Jesus.

The progress of God's work was most conspicuous in relation to revenge and warfare. The two high chiefs, Namakei and Naswai, frequently declared, "We are men of Christ now. We mustn't fight. We must put down murders and crimes among our people."

Two young fools, returning from Tanna with muskets, tried to shoot a man twice with no reason or provocation. The islanders met and warned them that if man or woman was injured by them, the other men would load their muskets and shoot them dead in public council. This was a mighty step toward public order, and I rejoiced in the Lord.

9

The Well

The sinking of a well broke the back of dark religion on Aniwa. Living on a flat coral island with little rain, Aniwa's islanders drank very unwholesome water at certain seasons. The best water they ever had was from the precious coconut. They also cultivated the sugarcane. To quench thirst, they would chew it. When they went off to the field for a day's work, they would take four or five sticks of sugarcane for their food and drink. With the sea as their bathtub, almost waterless cooking, and no clothes to be washed, the lack of fresh springwater was a worse trial for us than for the Aniwans.

I set up two large casks as cisterns for rainwater. But when we attempted to fill them at the village water hole, the islanders forbade us, fearing that our large casks wouldn't leave any water for their coconut bottles. This public water hole was on the ground of two sacred men who claimed the power of filling it by rain. Islanders gave them presents to bring rain. If it came soon, they took all the credit for it. If not, they demanded larger gifts to satisfy their gods. Even our Aneityumese teachers questioned my protests. "It is hard to know, Missi. The water does come

135

and go quickly. If you paid them well, they might bring the rain and let us fill our casks!"

I resolved with God's help to sink a well near the mission house. I prayed that a wisdom higher than my own would guide me to the source of a pure spring. I figured I would have to dig through earth and coral over thirty feet. I constantly feared that even if I found water, it would be salty! One morning I said to Chief Namakei and another chief, both earnestly learning about Jesus, "I am going to sink a deep hole into the earth to see if our God will send us fresh water up from below."

They looked at me with astonishment and said in a tone of pity, "O Missi! Wait till the rain comes down, and we will save all we possibly can for you."

"If no fresh water can be gotten, we may be forced to leave you."

The old chief looked imploringly, "O Missi! You must not leave us for that! Rain comes only from above. How could you expect our island to send us showers of rain from below?"

I tried to explain, "Fresh water does come springing up from the earth in my homeland, and I hope to see it here too."

He grew tender in his tones, "O Missi, you are losing something, or you would not talk wild like that! Don't let our people hear you talking about going down into the earth for rain, or they will never listen to your word or believe you again."

First, I selected a spot near the mission station and close to the public path so that it would be as useful as possible to everyone. I began to dig, using pick and spade, bucket, an American axe, and soon a ladder. The good old chief now had his men watch me in shifts so that I would not try to take my own life or do anything else in madness. "Poor Missi!" he said. "That's the way with all who go mad. There's no driving an idea out of their heads. We must watch him now. He will find it harder to work with pick and spade than with his pen. When he's tired we'll persuade him to give it up."

I did get exhausted under that tropical sun sooner than I had expected. So I went into the house and filled my vest pocket with large beautiful English-made fishhooks. These are very tempting to the young men for their superiority over their handmade shell hooks. Holding one up I called, "One of these to every man who fills and turns over three buckets out of this hole!"

They rushed for the first turn and back again and again for another. I kept those on one side who had gotten a turn till all the rest had a chance, and bucket after bucket was filled and emptied rapidly. Still the shaft seemed to lower too slowly while my fishhooks were disappearing very quickly. I was thankful when one evening we reached twelve feet deep, but by the next morning one side had fallen in, and all our work was undone.

The old chief and his best men now came around me more earnestly than ever. He assured me for the fiftieth time that rain would not come up through the earth on Aniwa! "Had you been in that hole last night," he scolded me, "you would have been buried, and a man-of-war would have come from Queen 'Toria to ask for the Missi that lived here. We would say, 'He is down in that hole.' The captain would ask, 'Who killed him and put him down there?' We would have to say, 'He went down there himself!'

The captain would answer, 'Nonsense! Who ever heard of a white man going down into the earth to bury himself? You killed him! You put him there! Don't hide your bad conduct with lies!' Then he would bring out his big guns and shoot us and destroy our island in revenge. You are making your own grave, Missi—and ours too. Give up this mad freak, for no rain will be found by going down. Besides, all your fishhooks cannot tempt my men again to enter that hole. They don't want to be buried with you. Won't you give it up now?"

I said all I could to quiet his fears. I explained that this cave-in could have been prevented with simple precautions. By the help of God, I would persevere with or without help.

Wracking my brain, I became an on-the-spot engineer. We got two trees capable of sustaining a cross-tree between them. I sank them on each side firmly into the ground and passed a beam across them over the center of the shaft. On the beam I fastened a homemade pulley, passed a rope over the wheel, and tied my largest bucket to the end of the rope. Now I attacked the digging again, but at an angle so that the sides might not fall in again. From then on not one islander would enter the hole. I had to pick and dig till I was utterly exhausted. A teacher managed the dirt removal from above, hiring islanders with axes, knives, and such. They held on to the rope as they walked along the ground till the bucket rose to the surface. Then the teacher would pull it over, empty it, and lower it to me again. I rang a little bell when the bucket was full, and up they would pull. And so I struggled from day to day, my heart almost sinking with the sinking of the well. Twenty feet . . . twenty-five feet . . . thirty feet. "Living water, living water, living water," kept chiming through my soul like music from God as I hammered and dug away!

At thirty feet the earth and coral became damp. I felt we were nearing water. My soul had faith that God would open a spring for us, but side by side with this faith was a strange terror that the water would be salty. Even the highest experiences of the soul are so perplexing and mixed.

One evening I said to old Chief Namakei, "I think that Jehovah God will give us water tomorrow from that hole!"

"No, Missi, you will never see rain coming up from the earth. We are wondering what is to be the end of this mad work of yours. We expect daily, if you do reach water, to see you drop through into the sea. Then the sharks will eat you! That will be the end of it—death to you and danger to us all!"

"Come tomorrow," I answered. "I hope and believe that Jehovah God will send rainwater up through the earth." At the moment I knew I was risking much, and perhaps incurring sorrowful consequences, if no water were given. Yet I had faith that the Lord was leading me on, and I knew that I sought His glory, not my own.

Next morning I went down again at daybreak and sank a narrow hole in the center about two feet deep. The perspiration broke over me with uncontrollable excitement, and I trembled through every limb as water rushed up and began to fill the hole. Muddy as it was, I eagerly tasted it, and the little tin cup dropped from my hand with sheer joy. It was water! It was fresh water! It was living water from Jehovah's well!

After a few moments, when I had praised the Lord, and my excitement was a little calmed, the mud had greatly settled. I filled a jug which I had taken down empty in the sight of all of them and ascended to the top. I called for them to come and see the rain that Jehovah God had given us through the well. They crowded around me and gazed on the jug in superstitious fear. The old chief shook it to see if it would spill. Then he touched it to see if it felt like water. At last he tasted it. Rolling it in his mouth with joy for a moment, he swallowed it and shouted, "Rain! Rain! Yes, it is rain! But, Missi, how did you get it?"

"Jehovah my God gave it out of His own earth in answer to our labors and prayers."

"Missi, wonderful, wonderful is the work of your Jehovah God! No god of Aniwa ever helped us in this way. Missi"—and he paused—"will it always rain up through the earth? Or will it come and go like the rain from the clouds?" I told them that I believed it would always be there as a gift from Jehovah.

"Missi," he went on, "will you and your family drink it all, or will we also have some?"

"You and all your people and all the people of the island may come and drink and carry away as much of it as you wish. The more of it we can use, the fresher it will be. That is the way with many of our Jehovah's best gifts."

"Missi, what can we do to help you now?"

"You have seen it fall in once already." "If it falls again, it will cover the rain from below which God has given us. In order to preserve it for us and for our children in all time, we must build it round and round with great coral blocks from the bottom to the very top. I will now clear it out and prepare the foundation for this wall of coral rock. Let everyone carry the largest blocks they can from the shore."

Scarcely were my words repeated when they all rushed to the shore with shouting and singing. Soon every one was seen struggling under the biggest block of coral he dared to tackle. They lay like limestone rocks, broken up by the hurricanes and rolled ashore in the arms of mighty billows. In an incredibly short time scores of them were lying around the mouth of the well. I received and placed each stone in its position, doing my poor best to wedge them one against another, building circularly, and cutting them to shape with my American axe. They took over for the last ten feet, working with all their hearts, some carrying, some cutting, till the wall rose like magic, with a row of the hugest rocks round the top. All wished to have a hand in building it, and it remains to this day, a solid wall of masonry, thirty-four feet deep, eight feet wide at the top and six at the bottom, with three-foot walls all around.

I built a wood floor over the mouth and fixed the bucket and windlass. There it stands as one of God's greatest blessings to Aniwa. An Aniwan said to me recently, "But for the well water during the last two years of drought, we would all have been dead." The water rises and falls with the tide, though a third of a mile from the sea, and is just a little salty at low tide. After becoming used to this water, the pure fresh water on board the *Dayspring* was so insipid that I slipped a little salt into my tea along with the sugar before I could enjoy it.

The islanders have since tried to sink six or seven wells near their various villages. They have either come to coral rock that they could not pierce or found saltwater. They say, "Missi not only used pick and spade, but he prayed and cried to his God. We have learned to dig but not how to pray, and therefore Jehovah will not give us the rain from below!"

When the well was finished and fenced in, old Chief Namakei said to me, "Missi, I think I could help you next Sunday. Will you let me preach a sermon on the well?"

"Yes," I replied at once, "if you will try to bring all the people to hear you."

The news spread like wildfire that Chief Namakei was to be the missionary on the next day of worship. Sunday dawned and Aniwa assembled a great crowd. Namakei appeared dressed in shirt and kilt. I conducted short opening devotions and then called on Namakei. He rose at once, his eyes flashing wildly, his limbs twitching with emotion. Swinging his tomahawk for emphasis, he began:

> Friends of Namakei, men and women and children of Aniwa, listen to my words! Since Missi came here he has talked many strange things we could not understand—things all too wonderful. We said they must be lies. White people might believe such nonsense, but the black fellow knew better. Of all his wonderful stories, the strangest was about sinking down through the earth to get rain! Then we said to each other, 'He's gone mad.' But the Missi prayed on and worked on, telling us that Jehovah God heard and saw; his God would give him rain. Was he mad? Has he not got the rain deep down in the

earth? We mocked him, but the water was there all the same. We have laughed at other things that the Missi told us because we could not see them. But from this day I believe that all he tells us about his Jehovah God is true. Someday our eyes will see it. For today we have seen the rain from the earth.

Then rising to a climax, he began to paw the ground like a great war horse, first one foot and then the other throwing the broken coral on the floor behind him. He cried with great eloquence:

My people, the people of Aniwa, the world is turned upside down since the word of Jehovah came to this land! Who ever expected to see rain coming up through the earth? It has always come from the clouds! Wonderful is the work of this Jehovah God. No god of Aniwa ever answered prayers as the Missi's God has done. Friends of Namakei, all the powers of the world could not have forced us to believe that rain could be given from the depths of the earth unless we had seen it with our eyes, felt it, and tasted it. Now, by the help of Jehovah God the Missi brought that invisible rain to view, which we had never heard nor seen.

Beating his hand on his breast, he exclaimed:

Something here in my heart tells me that the Jehovah God does exist, the Invisible One, whom we had not heard nor seen till the Missi brought Him to our knowledge. The coral has been removed, the land has been cleared away, and see, the water rises. Invisible till this day, yet all the time it was there; our eyes were too weak. So I, your chief, do now firmly believe that when I die, though this world now blinds my old eyes, I will then see the Invisible Jehovah God with my soul, as Missi tells me I will, as surely as I have seen the rain from the earth below.

From this day, my people, I must worship the God who has given us the well, and who fills us with rain from under the ground. The gods of Aniwa cannot hear, cannot help us, like the God of Missi. Henceforth, I am a follower of Jehovah God. Let every man that agrees with me go now and fetch the idols of Aniwa, the gods that our fathers feared, and throw them down at Missi's feet. Let us burn and bury and destroy these things of wood and stone. Let us have Missi teach us how to serve the God who can hear, the Jehovah who gave us the well, and who will give us every other blessing. He will give us all we need for He sent His Son Jesus to die for us and bring us to heaven. This is what the Missi has been telling us every day since he landed on Aniwa. We laughed at him, but now we believe him. The Jehovah God has sent us rain from the earth. Why wouldn't He send us His Son from heaven? Namakei stands up for Jehovah!

This message and the sinking of the well broke the back of dark religion on Aniwa. That very afternoon the old chief and several of his people brought their idols and threw them down at my feet beside the door of our house. What intense excitement in the weeks that followed! Group after group came to our door, loaded with their gods of wood and stone, and piled them up in heaps. Some were crying and others shouting, "Jehovah! Jehovah!" Whatever would burn we threw in a fire. Others we buried in pits twelve or fifteen feet deep. A few, more likely to awaken superstition, we sank far out in the sea.

Two sacred men and some other selected persons were appointed as a detective committee. They investigated and exposed those who pretended to give up their idols but were still hiding some. And they encouraged waverers to come to a thorough decision for Jehovah.

They flocked around us now at every meeting we held. They listened eagerly to the story of the life and death of Jesus. After three years on Aniwa we had our first baptism and communion. Beginning with the old chief, twelve converts came forward, and I baptized them one by one. Two of them had little children, and I baptized them too, as the first lambs of the flock.

At the moment when I put the bread and wine into those hands, once stained with the blood of cannibalism, now stretched out to Jesus, I had a foretaste of the joy of heaven that almost burst my heart in pieces. I will never taste a deeper bliss till I gaze on the glorified face of Jesus himself.

They watched our family and imitated our habits regarding morning and evening family prayer, grace at meals, and stopping ordinary work on the Lord's Day. Homes were identified as Christian or not on the basis of family prayer. All ordinary occupations ceased on Sundays. Saturday came to be known as cooking day since extra preparations were made for the day of worship.

Each village built its own school, which doubled as a church on Sundays. The Aneityumese teachers taught in the two most advanced schools, and the others were taught by the best readers I could find.

I rotated them frequently, returning them to our own school for a time. To encourage them, they received a small annual salary.

Everything was rapidly becoming "new" under the influence of Jesus. Almost everyone now attended school, sometimes with three generations at one copy of an alphabet book. Thefts, quarrels, and crimes were no longer settled by angry clubs, but by fines or bonds or the lash, as decided by the chiefs and their people. Industry increased. Huts and plantations were safe; before, every man carried all his valuables with him whenever he left home. Even a brood of fowl or a litter of pigs would be carried along. This made for lively episodes at church: chicks, piglets, and puppies all talking together as we sang, prayed, and preached! Now people could leave things safe and secure at home.

Though no one was compelled to come to church, every person on Aniwa, without exception, became a professing worshiper of Jehovah God!

At dawn on Monday the *tavaka* (canoe drum) sounded in every village on Aniwa. All inhabitants came to school for an hour and a half before the sun dried up the heavy dew, and then they were off to their plantations.

I spent my forenoon in translating, printing, visiting the sick, or whatever was most urgent. About two o'clock the islanders returned from their work, bathed in the sea, and dined on coconut or breadfruit. At three o'clock the mission bell would ring, and the afternoon school began. My wife and I taught the Aneityumese teachers and the more advanced students for about an hour and a half. After this the islanders spent their time in fishing, relaxing, or preparing supper—their main meal. Toward sundown the *tavaka* sounded again, and the day closed with the echoes of village prayers from under the banyan trees. This was our pattern day after day and week after week on Aniwa.

I often said I would not leave the islands again unless compelled to by a breakdown in health or the loss of the mission ship. From January to April 1873, the *Dayspring* was wrecked, we lost a darling child by death, my dear wife suffered a long illness, and I was brought very low with severe rheumatic fever. The captain of a visiting ship saw me and then told our fellow missionaries on Tanna that I was probably dead by then. They started at once in their open boat, rowing and sailing thirty miles to help us. A few days before they arrived I had fallen into a long sleep but had awakened conscious again. I was on the mend, but my weakness kept me using crutches for a long while.

Under orders to seek medical help and a change of climate, we set off. On our way, we began raising money for a replacement ship, holding meetings in Sydney, Victoria, and Melbourne. In New Zealand God gave me a heavenly dream or vision of music, brilliant angels, and a silhouette of the Lord Jesus, which greatly comforted me. After several months of meetings, God provided the needed money. And so our second *Dayspring* sailed on her annual trip to the islands, and we returned in her. We praised the Lord with reinvigorated bodies and spirits.

———

The second-highest chief on Aniwa was Nerwa, a keen debater. When I could speak a little in their language, I visited and preached at his village, but the moment he discovered that Jehovah's teaching opposed their religious customs, he sternly forbade us. During one sermon, he angrily interrupted me, "It's all lies you come here to teach us, and you call it worship! You say your Jehovah God dwells in heaven. Who ever went up there to see Him? Why, you cannot even climb one of our coconut trees, though we can easily! To climb onto the roof of your house, you need a ladder. If you could make your ladder higher than our highest coconut tree, what would you lean it against? When you got to its top you could only climb down the other side and end up where you started! The thing is impossible. You never saw God. You never heard Him speak. Don't come here with any of your white lies, or I'll send my spear through you."

He drove us from his village and furiously threatened murder if we ever dared to return. Soon after, the Lord sent us a little orphan girl from Nerwa's village. She learned to read and write quickly and told her villagers everything we taught her. Next an orphan boy was sent from that village, and he too took back stories of how kindly Missi the man and Missi the woman treated him. One day the chief's wife came to worship and said, "Nerwa's opposition is dying fast. The stories of the orphans do it. He has allowed me to attend church and to get the Christian's book." We gave her a book and a bit of clothing.

Woman after woman followed her from that same village, and some of the men began to come with them. The only part of worship they showed real interest in, however, was the children's singing.

At last Nerwa got so interested that he came

and sat outside within earshot of the music. Soon
he came close enough to hear our preaching. Then
he began openly coming in to worship. He weighed
and compared everything he heard and soon out-
distanced nearly all the Aniwans in his understanding of the Gospel. He professed himself a follower of the Lord Jesus and eagerly worked to bring
in a neighboring chief and his people.

I have seen him clasping the Bible like a living
thing to his breast and cry, "O to have this treasure
in my own words of Aniwa!" When Matthew and
Mark were printed at last in Aniwan, he studied
them incessantly. He became the teacher in his own
village school and an elder in the church.

Years later, when Nerwa was facing death, he
prayed for everyone who came to visit him and sang
with most of them. On my last visit to him, he drew
me near his face and whispered, "Missi, my Missi, I
am glad to see you. You see that group of young men?
They came to sympathize with me, but they have
never once spoken the name of Jesus, though they
have spoken about everything else! Read me the
story of Jesus. Pray for me to Jesus. No! Let's call
them, and let me speak with them before I go."

I called the young men all around him, and he
strained to talk to them, "After I am gone, let there
be no bad talk, no old ways. Sing Jehovah's songs,
and pray to Jesus, and bury me as a Christian. Take
good care of my Missi, and help him all you can. I am
dying happy and going to be with Jesus, and it was
Missi that showed me this way. Who among you will
take my place in the village school and in the church?
Who among you all will stand up for Jesus?"

Many were shedding tears, but no one replied,

and so the dying chief continued, "Now let my last work on earth be this: We will read a chapter of the Book, one verse each, and then I will pray for you all, and the Missi will pray for me, and God will let me go while the song is still sounding in my heart!"

After the Scripture reading and prayer, we gathered the Christians who were nearby and sang a hymn very softly in Aniwan, "There Is a Happy Land." As they sang, the old man grasped my hand and tried hard to speak, but he could not. Then his head fell to one side, and he was gone.

———

Litsi, the only daughter of Chief Namakei, became a bright, clever, and attractive Christian girl. Many men sought her hand, but she disdainfully told me, "I am queen of this island, and when I like I will ask a husband in marriage, as you said the great Queen Victoria did!"

Her first husband was undoubtedly the tallest and most handsome man on Aniwa, but he was a fool. On his early death, she returned to live with us at the mission house. Her second husband, Mungaw, was a fine man. Heir to a chief, he had been trained with us and loved Jesus. They were married in the church and lived happily together. He was a good speaker and was chosen as a deacon in the church, next an elder, and then high chief over half the island. After two armed men tried to kill him, he gave them a peace offering to show them real forgiveness. But when I took him with me to Australia once, he was kidnapped and drugged. Afterward he was given to violent fits of rage. In the end Nasi, a Tannese chief on Aniwa, executed Mungaw for insanity.

After a while, Queen Litsi was happily married again. She had a strong desire to go as a missionary to the people and tribe of Nasi, the very man who had murdered her second husband, on Tanna. She used to say, "Is there no missionary to go and teach Nasi's people? I weep and pray for them that they too may come to know and love Jesus."

"Litsi," I replied, "if I had only wept and prayed for you, but stayed at home in Scotland, would that have helped you know and love Jesus like you do?"

"Certainly not," she said.

"Litsi, wouldn't it please Jesus and be a grand and holy revenge if you, the Christians of Aniwa, carried the Gospel to the people whose chief murdered Mungaw?" The idea seized her soul. As soon as a missionary went to Nasi's people, Litsi and her husband led a small band of Aniwan Christians to serve as teachers with the missionary. There she has labored ever since. Her son is being trained by his cousin to be "the good chief of Aniwa," as she calls him in her prayers. She cries to God to bless and watch over him while she is serving the Lord in the mission field. She has served there many years now, and when I visited Tanna, she ran to me and kissed my hand. Sobbing, she cried, "O my father! God has blessed me to see you again. Is my mother, your dear wife, well? And your children, my brothers and sisters? My love to them all! Oh, my heart clings to you!"

As we talked she opened her heart. "My days are hard. I could be happy and rich as queen on Aniwa. But the lost are beginning to listen. What a reward when we will hear them sing and pray to our dear Savior! That hope makes me strong for anything."

Life, any life, would be well spent, under any

conceivable conditions, in bringing one human soul to know and love and serve God and His Son, and thereby securing for yourself at least one temple where your name and memory would be held forever and forever in affectionate praise—a regenerated heart in heaven. That fame will prove *immortal,* when all the poems and monuments and pyramids of Earth have gone into dust.

My adopted home church in Victoria, together with the missionaries, commissioned me to go home to Britain in 1884. They authorized me to work for a new mission ship, a sailing ship with a steam engine for back-up power. While at home I tried to speak at three churches each Sunday, one each weeknight, and at home meetings in the afternoon. I was privileged to speak at the home of Charles Spurgeon, the famous preacher, and at the orphanages of George Mueller, the great man of prayer. Often as I have looked at the doings of men and churches and tried to bring all to the test as if in Christ's very presence, it has seemed to me that such work as Mueller's must be especially dear to the heart of our Lord. Were He to visit this world now and look for a place where His Spirit's work is fully done, I fear that many of our churches would be passed by. His holy, tender, helpful love would find its most perfect reflex in these orphan homes. This, *this,* is "pure and undefiled religion" before God the Father!

I returned to Australia with half again more than what was needed for the sail/steamship. The extra was set aside for supporting new missionaries. It has been the dream of my life to see one missionary on every one of the islands of Vanuatu. Then I could lie down and gladly whisper, "Lord, let Your servant now depart in peace!"

10

Around the World and Home Again

From 1886 to 1892 my days were divided between Australia and New Zealand with visits to the islands of Vanuatu. God has used the story of our mission work to recruit missionaries for lost peoples around the world.

On the advice of the British government, my Australian church sent me to America in 1892 to persuade the United States government to ban trade in alcohol, opium, and firearms throughout the islands. When Great Britain prohibited all her own traders from bartering with alcohol and firearms in the South Pacific islands, her traders had protested loudly. They found themselves handicapped in that French and American competitors faced no such prohibition. France professed willingness to accept the same prohibition if America would. I was also sent to represent my church at the Pan-Presbyterian Council in Toronto, to recruit missionaries, and to raise support.

We sailed into San Francisco in September and went on to the Council in Toronto by rail. After the convention many churches in the United States invited me to come and speak. I asked every meeting, except those on Sundays, to forward petitions to the President and Congress, calling for the prohibition of bartering with intoxicants and firearms in Vanuatu. The newspapers printed all these petitions, and the public became interested.

By God's direction, on my second Sunday in Washington, D.C., I preached to President Benjamin Harrison, himself, and many senators and representatives. The President declared himself willing to expedite the negotiations with Britain in every possible way. He sent word to the British government that the United States would cooperate in prohibiting bartering with intoxicants and firearms in Vanuatu. But the British reply added an exception clause that he disapproved of. Before President Harrison could reach agreement with Britain, President Grover Cleveland was installed at the White House.

President and Mrs. Cleveland invited me to lunch at the White House, privately, to question me regarding the islanders and our work. They seemed to be genuine followers of the Savior and sincerely interested in the salvation of the lost. President Cleveland expressed himself as deeply interested, but the final reply from Britain was still delayed.

Once back in London I learned that Britain had stalled because France and Russia had withdrawn from the proposal. For years France had declared its agreement with the prohibition if America would sign on. Now, when America was ready, France withdrew!

Meanwhile I visited the leading cities of all the

northern states and a few southern cities also. My next goal was to return to Canada. I commonly addressed two or three meetings daily with long distances between. Each Sunday I spoke at three to seven meetings. It was dreadfully exhausting, but time was short. During one period I addressed ten meetings per day and some weeks even more. But the time came to say farewell to Canada and the United States.

My arrival in Britain was amazingly different from ten years before. Then I had gone from minister to minister, often pleading in vain for a chance to speak to their churches. Now I was no longer treated as a stranger, but as a dear friend of everyone who had read the first two parts of my book. During the two years of my tour I addressed almost fourteen hundred audiences, ranging from a few hundred people to six thousand. I spoke to tradesmen, archbishops, and dukes.

I never felt more deeply humbled than at the close of some of those unparalleled meetings when I was alone with my Savior after all had gone home. I thought of my lowly home and all the paths where the God of my father had led me from hardship to this day of triumph. Fame and influence laid me lower and yet lower at the feet of Jesus. I felt it the most deeply when I was speaking to professors and students at the sixty-three universities and theological schools where I was invited, including the universities of Princeton, Oxford, Edinburgh, Cambridge, and Glasgow.

I had visited Britain ten years earlier for the express purpose of raising money for a new *Dayspring* with auxiliary steam power. God had supplied, but disagreement had emerged back in Australia. Our mission ship would mean fewer passengers for the trading company shipping in our islands. Unwilling to give up that income, shipping officials and their church friends had discouraged getting the new ship. They convinced the church that it could not afford the annual maintenance the new ship would require and had prevented the ship's purchase for ten years now! Very quickly the churches in Britain provided the additional money needed for maintenance and more.

The new steam auxiliary *Dayspring* was built in Britain and exhibited to friends at Glasgow, Belfast, and Liverpool before setting out. Thousands flocked to see the little missionary ship and wish her Godspeed. On her first trip to Vanuatu the islanders thrilled at the sight of their own Gospel ship, and she carried supplies and missionaries for months. On her fourth trip, however, she struck an uncharted reef and plunged down into the sea. Thankfully, no lives were lost. This wreck was one of the bitterest sorrows of my life, and I wept at the loss of ten years of prayers and hard work. I was able to say, "The Lord gave and the Lord has taken away," but, God forgive me, it was very hard to add, "Blessed be the name of the Lord." Yet I know my Lord Jesus makes no mistakes! When we see all His meaning, we will understand what now we can only trustfully believe: that all is well.

———

My first Sunday back on Aniwa after a four-year absence gave me a happy surprise. Before daybreak I lay awake thinking of all my experiences on that island. I wondered whether the church had fallen off in my long absence, when suddenly I heard singing! It scarcely seemed to be dawn, but I jumped up and called to a man passing by, "Have I overslept? Is it already church time?"

He was one of their leaders and gravely replied, "Missi, since you left, we have found it very hard to live close to God! So the chief and the teachers and a few others meet every Sunday at daybreak and spend the first hour of the day in prayer. They are meeting to pray for you now that God may help you in your preaching, that all hearts may bear fruit today to the glory of Jesus."

I went back to my room and felt ready to preach. It would be an easy and joyful task to lead such a congregation into the presence of the Lord! They were already there!

That morning every person on Aniwa seemed to be at church. At the close of the services, the elders reported that they had kept up all the meetings during my absence. They had also conducted a new members' class and now presented me with their large group of candidates. When I saw the faithfulness of these poor Aniwan elders in teaching and serving during those four long years, my soul cried out to God, "What could the church accomplish if the elders in my homeland would serve Jesus like these saints, teaching the ignorant, protecting the tempted, and rescuing the fallen?"

We press forward still, never thinking we can lawfully rest until every tribe on these islands has heard, each in its mother tongue, the old and ever new and deathless story of Redeeming Love.

Now a missionary institute has been launched

in Vanuatu itself, at the very center of these cannibal islands. We pray daily that the Lord will send out consecrated native evangelists and pastors to guide the church of Vanuatu without European leadership. We eagerly look to that day, and then to go to other fields!

Let me record my immovable conviction that missions is the noblest service in which any human being can spend himself or be spent. If God gave me back my life to be lived over again, I would without one quiver of hesitation lay it on the altar to Christ for Him to use it as before in similar ministries of love, especially among those who have never heard the name of Jesus. Nothing I have endured makes me tremble when I ask the Lord to take my children to the mission field. I pray that He will open their way and make it their joy to live and die in carrying Jesus and His Gospel into the heart of a lost world. God gave His best, His Son, to me. I give back my best, my all, to Him.

Should the record of my poor and broken life lead any to consecrate themselves to mission work at home or abroad, or should it deepen the spirit of any missionaries, I bless and adore my beloved Master and Savior, to whom be glory forever.

Epilogue

J ohn Paton lived several years after writing the last portion of his autobiography. He settled his third son, Frank, on Tanna. The *Dayspring* was not replaced, but its remaining funds were given to work on the island of Malekula, where his second son, Fred, served. He printed the complete New Testament in Aniwan in 1899, and distributed it with the help of his daughter, Minnie.

In 1899, Paton's Australian church sent him to represent her at the World's Presbyterian Council, in Washington, D.C. While touring in the United States and Canada, he had a severe physical breakdown and was ordered to rest. Unwilling to rest except on a ship, he booked passage for Britain. There he rebelled against new orders to rest and preached in England, Scotland, and Northern Ireland for six months. At his farewell meeting in London, he exhorted the crowd of thousands, "If the church of God fully realized her heritage in the Gospel, she would send ten thousand fresh messengers to the farthest parts of the earth to proclaim Jesus."

He arrived back in Australia in July 1901, but was so ill that he was not given permission to return to Aniwa until April 1902, when he visited there with his wife for several months, They returned to Australia in early 1903. He went back to the islands for a four-month tour in 1904, but was called back to Australia for other duties after only two months out.

Mrs. Margaret Whitecross Paton died in her sleep, May 16, 1905. Her husband kept preaching around Australia. On the way to one church, the horse pulling his buggy spooked and threw the missionary headfirst to the ground. To the amazement of the congregation that evening, the white-haired Paton was helped into the pulpit with his head wrapped in bandages. He held on to the pulpit for support and poured out his heart to them.

In 1906 Paton pleaded to return to the islands, but the mission's medical advisers would not grant it. In early December he preached his final sermon. Two days later, in his last letter he wrote, "After three weeks' incessant work, and often traveling from fifteen to twenty miles by buggies and not getting to bed till between 1 and 2 A.M. . . . I broke down, as when last in Canada."

He asked his doctor a few days after Christmas, "Do you think I will be well enough to go to the islands in January?" But he would never travel or preach again. He began to sink rapidly and passed away on the twenty-eighth of January, 1907.